AfriCali

SIMON
ELEMENT

Simon Element
New York London Toronto Sydney New Delhi

Afri Cali

recipes from my jikoni

Kiano Moju

Photography by
Kristin Teig

Jikoni [Swahili]
noun: kitchen

To my mom, Katano:

My original taste-tester and eternal culinary cheerleader. From questionable concoctions to gourmet triumphs, thanks for always clearing the plate. This cookbook is dedicated to you!

contents

introduction

veggies

flatbreads, rice & friends

eggs, chicken & seafood

beef, lamb & pork

sweets & drinks

my jikoni

introduction

karibu africali

When someone learns that I cook,
the first question is always one of two:
"What's your signature dish?" or
"What kind of food do you cook?"
AfriCali really sums it all up. I was
born in Oakland, California, to a
Kenyan mother and a Nigerian father,
who both came to California as young
adults, having a split worldview
between their old home and new.

I spent many summer breaks in Kenya on my maternal grandparents' Maasai ranch. During the school year in California, I loved going to family-friendly African house parties, where there were huge foil catering trays of Nigerian jollof rice, moin moin (a steamed bean cake), roasted chicken legs, and plantains. During the school week, I would beg for strawberry Pop-Tarts, eat bean and cheese burritos for school lunch, and if I was lucky, my mom would pick up a Vietnamese clay pot (a rice takeout dish cooked in a clay pot, similar to a biryani) for dinner. On the weekends, we would make Kenyan dishes like ugali (cooked white cornmeal, similar to firm grits or polenta) and sukuma wiki (sautéed collard greens), or go to my uncle's house for nyama choma (barbecued meat) if someone had a birthday. The best treat would be going to the restaurant Asmara in Oakland for a platter of Ethiopian and Eritrean dishes. This isn't a recipe book of traditional recipes, but rather a book inspired by the tastes I grew up with and the delicious meals I've had thus far in life.

Californian cuisine is not necessarily about named dishes, but more an approach to cuisine.

California food culture embraces the flavors of its immigrant communities while celebrating the state's agriculture and the flavors of fresh produce. I bring that philosophy when cooking the dishes of Africa that I grew up eating and enjoyed while traveling.

If you're new to modern African cuisine, or simply seeking inspiration for food that feels like home, I hope this book will inspire you in new ways to use ingredients that are around you, or even already in your kitchen. It's easy to think that food inspired by places far away is a departure from what we know, but the truth is, we live in a global economy, where we have more similarities than differences, and yes, that applies to food, too.

Every day we eat ingredients with international origins that have become local staples. I feel confident that I can cook my food almost anywhere in the world with a decent-size grocery store. Sure, there may be a substitution here and there, but those variations can make for the most delicious meals.

Oh, and I've never had a signature dish, because life is too short to obsess over one plate of food!

kiano cooks

I'm not sure if anyone can explain why we're drawn to certain things, but for me, it's always been cooking. My mother would make Kenyan meals on the weekends, and while making chapati, she would break off a small piece of dough for me to play with, fully expecting me to get bored and move on to toys. But as the insistent toddler I was, I wanted my dough to look like Mom's. That meant my tiny piece of dough had to be rolled out and cooked just like hers. I guess it's a phase I never grew out of, constantly pestering my mom in the kitchen to let me cook. When she gifted me a toy oven that produced semiedible cakes, my obsession reached unforeseen levels, and I took on the role of pastry chef for every family meal, trying to force-feed my family these tiny cakes that were cooked under a light bulb. It was that following summer that I enrolled in my first cooking camp.

As I was tall for a seven-year-old, I had no problem reaching the kitchen counters to prepare a plethora of California-style dishes. Raised in the East Bay of the San Francisco Bay Area, I ate it all, and in the camp, we cooked it all! Spring rolls, agua frescas (fruit punch), and lots of fresh produce that reflected California.

When I was finally given permission to cook unsupervised, I would quietly wake up early on the weekends to sit inches away from the TV on low volume as the public television station played the early morning cooking shows. I would then go into the kitchen to make a recipe from my *Children's World Cookbook*, talking to my imaginary audience about bowls and kitchen utensils and teaching them how to make today's dish.

I never stopped cooking at home; taking recreational classes, designing and printing menus for family dinners, or dreaming of a career in food. I did a semester abroad in London in my junior year at Syracuse University. I was an active member of the school cooking club, kicking off my obsession with tea cakes and moderately sweet desserts. But it was my photography class that gave me the knowledge and encouragement to start my first food blog.

I carried on blogging all the way through grad school. Feeling encouraged by friends who, in social settings, introduced me as a food blogger and by readers who would share when they made one of my dishes for a loved one, it was a success! My blog was never big, but it was enough to encourage me to pursue a career where I could create and share recipes.

I returned to London for my publishing master's degree at the University of the Arts, London, to learn how to do this as a professional career. This time around, I really got to enjoy the city's global food scene, interning at a cooking school and a food magazine, and eating £5 lunch plates from cooks across the globe. I even had a pop-up restaurant, Orange St., where I served tacos inspired by the foods I ate in the Bay. By the end of the term, I had coauthored my first cookbook as a school project, where we cooked and photographed everything in my Shoreditch dorm.

Kiano in middle school

Just as I handed in my thesis on the rise of online recipe videos, I got my first industry job offer that brought me back to California to produce cooking videos for Tasty, BuzzFeed's food channel, which would go on to garner tens of millions of views.

I now run my kitchen studios, Jikoni Studios, in Los Angeles. It's a culinary creative space where folks from food-related industries come to shoot their food photography and cooking videos. We host cooking classes that bring in cooks from cultures traditionally underrepresented in the restaurant and food media industry, giving people a hands-on educational experience. Jikoni Studios is where I write all my recipes, shoot my videos, host friends and family for brunches, and, of course, where we shot this book! It's my culinary playground that has helped me materialize all my ideas. I think I cook more here than I do at home!

my approach to cooking

As much as I love to cook, I've always been drawn to unfussy recipes while maintaining a dedication to flavor.

A recipe with a long ingredient list can come off as intimidating or be perceived as more difficult. This is probably why so many publishers favor recipes that are short and sweet but, in many cases, are tasteless. This is where my little cheats come in. The way I see it, if my fridge and pantry are never without delicious little things, then there's no way the meals made in this kitchen could ever come out flat. So, in this cookbook, you'll see a fair amount of references to spice blends and other delicious things. That way, your labor for today's meals will bear fruit for the whole week!

Cooking with exactness is not the culinary philosophy I was raised under. A cooking philosophy shared between Africa and its diaspora is a sensory approach to cooking. Most cooks in my family are full by the time the meal is done just from tasting along the way. Clean hands are the best tool for cooking (and eating), so you can build that familiarity with what things should feel like to guide you in the kitchen.

how to use this book

The ingredient list should read like a shopping list. For the most part, the ingredient preparation is in the instructions, and they are written with great consideration for being efficient in the kitchen. That means you'll be boiling that pot of water while you chop the vegetables, or the sauce will cook down while you prepare the remaining ingredients.

Pressure should have no place in a home kitchen. Rarely will I bail on making a dish because I'm missing a few ingredients, and some ingredients are intentionally left open to what you have at home. If a dish calls for an onion, use whichever you have. Chances are that the difference it would make in the recipe is so subtle that it's not worth the extra shopping trip.

I prefer using the grams measurement where available—especially when baking—as a kitchen scale doesn't take up much space, and I find it much quicker to use than measuring cups.

veggies

cauliflower bhajias

Let's be real. The best way to eat cauliflower is fried. As the East African cousin to Indian pakoras, bhajias are fried potatoes coated in spiced chickpea flour. Creating odd shapes makes for better bhajias, as there are more nooks and crevices for the soon-to-be crispy batter to cling to.

1 medium head cauliflower

1 teaspoon coriander seeds

2 fresh medium hot chili peppers, such as serrano or Fresno

Handful fresh cilantro

Neutral oil, such as avocado or peanut oil, for frying

⅓ cup chickpea flour

¼ cup cornstarch

1 tablespoon Garlic Ginger Paste (page 231)

Fine sea salt

Sea salt flakes

Lemon wedges, for serving

1 Cut the florets off the cauliflower and break them into 1-inch pieces. Cut the stalk into ½-inch pieces. Set aside.

2 With a mortar and pestle or a rolling pin, roughly crush the coriander seeds. Finely chop the chili peppers (remove the seeds for a milder flavor) and cilantro (both leaves and stems) and transfer to a mixing bowl.

3 Fill a medium heavy-bottom pot with 2 inches of oil, and heat over medium-high until the oil reaches 350°F (180°C). Line a plate with paper towels and place it beside the stove.

4 While the oil heats, to the mixing bowl with the coriander seeds, chili peppers, and cilantro, add the chickpea flour, cornstarch, garlic ginger paste, and 1 teaspoon fine sea

salt. Whisk everything together and slowly pour in some water, a few tablespoons at a time, until the batter is slightly runny and has a few lumps. Be careful not to add too much water or the batter will become too runny; if this happens, add extra chickpea flour, a teaspoon at a time, until the batter thickens again.

5 Coat a few cauliflower pieces in the batter and shake off any excess. Fry the cauliflower pieces in the hot oil, and cook in batches to not overcrowd the pan, frequently turning the pieces until they are golden brown, 2 to 3 minutes on each side.

6 Remove and place on the paper towel–lined plate, and immediately season with sea salt flakes to taste. Serve warm with lemon wedges.

charred cabbage

If you think about it, cabbage is just a giant Brussels sprout. You get a delectably crispy exterior and a tender, slightly sweet interior when cooked in a lot of fat. Depending on how indulgent I feel, I will prepare this on the stovetop or in the oven. The oven requires less fat, but you can baste the cabbage in butter between each layer on the stove.

1 small head green cabbage

2 tablespoons extra-virgin olive oil, plus more as needed

Fine sea salt

Freshly ground black pepper

4 tablespoons (½ stick) unsalted butter (for stovetop method)

Herby Harissa (page 228)

1 Slice through the stem of the cabbage and cut the cabbage into 4 wedges; if the cabbage is on the larger side, it may need to be cut into 6 to 8 wedges. Coat all sides with the 2 tablespoons oil and season with salt and black pepper.

Stovetop Method

2 Heat a wide cast-iron skillet over medium-high heat. Once hot (sprinkle a few drops of water into the pan—the water should sizzle and evaporate quickly), lightly coat the bottom of the pan with oil. Arrange the cabbage wedges in the pan, leaving a small space between them. Allow the cabbage to slightly char on the bottom before turning. Cook until the cabbage is tender and easily pierced with a knife, 5 to 7 minutes on each side.

3 Reduce the heat to medium-low. Turn the wedges so the layers face upward and add the butter to the pan. Tilt the pan toward you so all the melted butter pools in one area, and using a spoon, scoop up the butter and baste the cabbage wedges; the hot butter will fall between the cabbage layers. Do this for about 2 minutes, being careful not to burn the butter.

4 Remove from the heat. Transfer the wedges to a serving dish, and spoon the herby harissa on top. Serve with the remaining herby harissa on the side.

Oven Method

2 Place the oven rack two shelves down from the top. Set the broiler to medium-high heat. Line a baking sheet with foil and arrange the cabbage wedges in the pan.

3 Broil for 10 minutes, then flip, and cook the other side for another 10 minutes. The cabbage is ready when the edges are slightly charred and it's easily pierced with a knife. Transfer the wedges to a serving dish, and spoon the herby harissa on top. Serve warm with extra herby harissa on the side.

chickpeas in coconut sauce

When it comes to curries, there are two main classes: aromatic curries, common in Thailand, and spice curries, common in India. The curries found on the East African coast seem to balance the two, where aromatics are sizzled with a conservative amount of spice before swimming in creamy coconut milk. This recipe can work with any canned bean or lentil and is best enjoyed with rice or flatbread.

2 (14-ounce) cans chickpeas

1 medium onion

1 medium green bell pepper

¼ cup avocado or coconut oil

4 green onions

2 tablespoons Garlic Ginger Paste (page 231)

1 teaspoon cumin seeds

3 tablespoons tomato paste

2 teaspoons garam masala

2 teaspoons chili flakes

1 teaspoon sweet paprika

½ teaspoon ground turmeric

Fine sea salt

1 (14-ounce) can coconut milk

1 cup chicken or vegetable stock

Handful fresh cilantro

Chapati (see pages 64 and 68), grains, or any kind of flatbread, for serving

1 Drain and rinse the chickpeas. Set aside. Finely chop the onion and place into a small bowl. Finely chop the bell pepper and add to the same bowl.

2 Heat the avocado oil in a large pot or Dutch oven over medium-high heat. When the oil is shimmering, add the onion and bell pepper, and cook, stirring occasionally, until the onion has softened and is lightly golden on the edges, 3 to 4 minutes. Meanwhile, thinly slice the green onions.

3 Add the green onions, garlic ginger paste, and cumin seeds to the pot, and cook, stirring frequently, until fragrant, 2 to 3 minutes.

4 Stir in the tomato paste, garam masala, chili flakes, paprika, turmeric, and 1 teaspoon salt, and cook, stirring occasionally, until the tomato paste darkens, 2 to 3 minutes.

5 Slowly stir in the coconut milk until the tomato paste dissolves. Then stir in the chickpeas and chicken stock. Season with salt to taste, allow to come to a simmer, and cook uncovered for 10 minutes.

6 Roughly chop the cilantro (leaves and stems). When ready to serve, turn off the heat, and stir in the cilantro, reserving a few leaves for garnish. Serve in bowls garnished with the reserved cilantro leaves, and enjoy with the chapati, grains, or any kind of flatbread.

Spice
Coconut
Harissa

grilled corn salad

I first made this salad on a roof deck in Mombasa, the port city of Kenya's coastline. The summers in Mombasa are hot and sticky, but as the evening breeze sets in, it's nice to start a jiko (portable charcoal stove) and cook supper outside. The corn just needs a good char, which can be achieved indoors using a cast-iron pan, or, my favorite way when the weather is right: on the grill. I encourage as many meals as possible to be prepared outdoors.

For the Salad Dressing

1 fresh medium hot chili pepper, such as serrano or Fresno

1 garlic clove

½ lemon

Fine sea salt

2 tablespoons extra-virgin olive oil

For the Salad

2 ears corn

2 tablespoons Peri-Peri Butter (page 232)

Juice of 1 lime

Fine sea salt

4 tightly packed cups arugula

1 small cucumber

1 avocado

Handful fresh basil

Handful fresh mint

1 **Make the salad dressing:** Cut the chili pepper in half lengthwise. Scrape out and discard the seeds for a milder flavor, then finely slice. Place into a small mixing bowl.

2 Using a Microplane, grate the garlic into the same bowl. Zest the lemon into the bowl, then add the lemon juice, being careful not to add the seeds. Season with salt, then carefully whisk in the oil. Set aside.

3 **Make the salad:** Heat a cast-iron pan or grill over high heat. If needed, remove the husks and corn silk from the corn cobs. Char the corn on all sides, turning frequently, for 10 to 15 minutes. Remove from the heat when charred to your preference.

4 Once cool enough to touch, cut off the corn kernels by standing the corn on the large end and cutting downward toward the cutting board. Place the corn in a large mixing bowl or serving bowl along with the peri-peri butter, and stir to melt the butter fully into the corn. Add the lime juice, season with salt to taste, and mix well.

5 Cut the arugula into 1-inch pieces. Cut the cucumber into a small dice, and cut the avocado into small chunks. Add to the bowl of corn. Discard the stems from the basil and mint, then tear the leaves into the bowl. When ready to serve, toss everything with the salad dressing, and transfer to a serving platter.

fried sweet plantains

Plantains are one of the first foods I was allowed to cook on my own. The most crucial step in this recipe is cooking the plantain at the correct ripeness. The best sweet plantains are typically dark yellow with plenty of black spotting. The flesh should be soft but not overly ripe when gently squeezed, like a mushy banana. Cutting the plantain into long slices gives you maximum surface area for browning, but in this recipe you can cut any shape of plantain your heart desires.

2 medium ripe plantains (soft, dark yellow with black spots)

Neutral oil, such as avocado or peanut oil, for frying

Sea salt flakes

1 Peel each plantain, cut it in half widthwise, then cut into long ¼-inch-thick slices. You can also slice them into rounds, cubes, or diagonal wedges.

2 Fill a pan with ¼ inch of oil and heat to 350°F (180°C). Line a plate with paper towels and place it beside the stove.

3 Once the oil is shimmering, test the temperature with a tiny end piece of plantain; it should immediately sizzle. If there is no sizzle, the oil is not hot enough. If it browns too quickly, the oil is too hot, and you should lower the heat.

4 Working in batches, shallow fry the plantains and cook to a golden brown, 3 to 5 minutes on each side. A fork is the best tool to turn the plantains without squishing them. Drain on the paper towel–lined plate and immediately season with salt flakes. Enjoy warm as a snack or as a side dish.

kachumbari salad

A salad interpretation of the famous East African condiment. Despite typically being made with Roma tomatoes, cherry tomatoes add a nice sweetness that balances out the hearty meat dishes this is commonly served with.

tip

Add other veggies such as thinly sliced cucumber, or lay the tomatoes on a bed of finely shredded green cabbage.

½ fresh medium hot chili pepper, such as serrano or Fresno

1 small garlic clove

2 tablespoons extra-virgin olive oil

Juice of ½ lemon

Fine sea salt

1 small red onion

Handful fresh cilantro

1 pound mixed-size salad tomatoes, such as heirloom, beefsteak, or cherry

1   Finely chop the chili pepper (remove the seeds for a milder flavor). Grate the garlic into a small bowl with a Microplane, and make a simple dressing by adding the chili pepper, oil, lemon juice, and salt to taste, mixing with a spoon or whisk to combine.

2   Thinly slice the onion into rings. Use a sieve or colander and rinse the onion rings under cold water. Drain and add to the salad dressing bowl to pickle in the dressing, mix well, and set aside.

3   Roughly chop the cilantro leaves. Slice the tomatoes into ½-inch rounds and season with salt, then arrange on a serving platter. This can be done up to 1 hour before you're ready to serve.

4   Use a fork to remove the onion from the dressing and arrange on top of the tomatoes. Pour the dressing over the salad platter, then garnish with the cilantro and serve immediately.

kale & egusi

Soups are at the heart of Nigerian cuisine. Traditional egusi soup takes a few hours to prepare; egusi is made from ground-up melon seeds combined with water to make a paste, then dolloped into an umami-rich broth with meat and greens. This quicker version pairs those signature flavors with California's favorite leafy green—kale.

The use of dried shellfish such as crayfish or shrimp is common in traditional Nigerian cooking, adding that umami and that signature Naija taste. Ground crayfish can be easily found in any West African grocery store or ordered online.

1 medium onion

3 tablespoons extra-virgin olive oil

1 medium red bell pepper

1 fresh very hot chili pepper, such as habanero or Scotch bonnet

2 teaspoons ground crayfish (optional)

1 bunch green kale

Fine sea salt

1 cup ground melon seeds (egusi) or pumpkin seeds

1⅓ cups chicken stock

1 teaspoon Curry Powder (page 239)

Any cooked protein, for serving

1 Finely dice the onion. Heat the oil in a large pot or Dutch oven over medium-high heat. When the oil starts to shimmer, add the diced onion and cook, stirring occasionally, until softened, 3 to 4 minutes.

2 While the onion cooks, roughly chop the bell pepper and chili pepper (remove the seeds for a milder spice), add to a blender, and blend until smooth. Add the mixture to the cooked onion along with the ground crayfish (if using), and stir to combine.

3 Reduce the heat to medium and cook, stirring occasionally, to prevent burning, until the water from the peppers evaporates and the mixture darkens, about 10 minutes.

4 Remove the thick stalks from the kale. Stack and roll the leaves tightly, then cut into ¼-inch-thick pieces. Add to the pot, season with a good pinch of salt, and stir to combine. Cook until the leaves wilt, stirring occasionally, about 10 minutes.

5 Combine the ground melon seeds in a small bowl with ¾ cup of chicken stock and ¼ teaspoon salt. Stir the remaining stock and the curry powder into the mixture in the pot, then slowly pour in the melon seed mixture. Do not stir. Cover with a lid and let the soup cook for 5 minutes. Season with salt to taste. Serve warm with any cooked protein.

tip
If you can't find melon seeds (egusi), pumpkin seeds are a great alternative and can either be bought ground or whole and then ground in a mortar and pestle.

peri-peri fried mushrooms

Light, crispy, and spicy, these fried oyster mushrooms can be enjoyed as a starter or as the star in a sandwich or wrap. Taking inspiration from peri-peri chicken, one of the most famous dishes to come out of southern Africa, there is no shying away from the spice here. Serve it alongside Herby Yogurt (page 226) for something cool.

tip

Enjoy these as a veggie alternative to a fried chicken sandwich.

2 bundles (roughly 8 ounces) oyster mushrooms

¾ cup cornstarch, divided

Neutral oil, such as avocado or peanut oil, for frying

¼ cup all-purpose flour

Fine sea salt

1 teaspoon sweet paprika

1 teaspoon garlic powder

1 teaspoon African bird's eye chili powder or cayenne pepper

1 teaspoon freshly ground black pepper

1 teaspoon baking powder

Sea salt flakes

Lime or lemon wedges, for serving

1   Break apart the mushrooms in 2-inch-wide pieces and place in a mixing bowl. Toss the mushrooms with ¼ cup of cornstarch, being sure to coat well.

2   Heat 2 inches of oil in a medium heavy-bottom pot over medium-high until it reaches 350°F (180°C). Line a plate with paper towels and place it beside the stove.

3   While the oil heats, in a separate bowl, whisk together the remaining ½ cup of cornstarch, the flour, 2 teaspoons salt, the paprika, garlic

powder, chili powder, black pepper, and baking powder. Slowly whisk in ⅔ cup water, making sure there are no lumps. The batter should be thin but not too runny.

4   Working with a few at a time to not overcrowd the pan, coat the mushrooms in the batter, shaking off any excess. Add the mushrooms to the hot oil and cook until golden brown, 3 to 4 minutes, turning midway. Remove and place on the paper towel–lined plate, and immediately season with the sea salt flakes. Serve warm with the lime wedges.

lentil nuggets

In West Africa, bean fritters are incredibly common. As a take on Nigerian akara, traditionally made with black-eyed peas that need to be skinned, these lentil fritters are light and airy and, best of all, require no skinning. Spooned into hot oil, these fritters take on a rough shape that resembles chicken nuggets.

tip
Fry just one nugget to check your seasoning and cook time before cooking up the whole batch.

1 cup red lentils

½ medium red onion

1 fresh very hot chili pepper, such as habanero or Scotch bonnet

½ medium red bell pepper

Handful fresh chives

Handful fresh cilantro

Handful fresh parsley

1 tablespoon (or one 10-gram cube, crushed) shrimp or chicken bouillon powder

½ teaspoon ground turmeric

Fine sea salt

Neutral oil, such as avocado or peanut oil, for frying

Mango Sweet Chili Sauce (page 226)

1 Soak the lentils in 3 cups water for at least 1 hour, or ideally 4 hours to overnight. Drain well.

2 Cut the onion into chunks. Remove the seeds from the chili pepper if you want a mild spice level. Add the onion, chili pepper, and lentils to a blender, and combine until the mixture is pale in color and completely smooth, scraping down the edges as needed. Scrape the mixture into a mixing bowl.

3 Finely dice the bell pepper and add to the bowl. Finely chop the chives, cilantro, and parsley (leaves and stems), and add to the bowl along with the shrimp bouillon powder, turmeric, and salt to taste and mix well to combine.

4 Fill a frying pan set over medium heat with a ¼ inch of oil. Line a plate with paper towels and place it beside the stove.

5 When the oil is shimmering, working in batches, fry the nuggets. Being sure to not overcrowd the pan, drop rounded tablespoons of batter into the hot oil, pressing them so they are ¼-inch thick, carefully leaving space between each nugget so they don't stick together. Once the bottoms are golden brown, 1 to 2 minutes, use a fork to carefully flip the nuggets over to finish cooking the other side, and fry until browned, another 1 to 2 minutes. Strain on the paper towel–lined plate and repeat with the remaining batter, adding more oil as needed. Serve warm with mango sweet chili sauce on the side.

lentil samosas

This veggie-friendly version of Kenyan samosas is made with lentils instead of beef. As they are already a labor of love, using precooked lentils helps save some time. You can prepare the samosas and freeze them after frying to have on hand for the perfect appetizer or snack.

FREEZING INSTRUCTIONS:
Arrange the cooked samosas in a single layer on a baking tray lined with parchment paper. Lightly wrap in plastic wrap and freeze until solid. Once solid, transfer them into a freezer-safe resealable bag. Keep frozen for up to 6 months. Reheat in the oven or air fryer, or quickly refry on the stove. Do not reheat in the microwave, or they will become soggy.

1½ cups cooked puy (French) or brown lentils (typically a 14-ounce can)

½ medium onion

3 green onions

2 garlic cloves or 1 tablespoon Garlic Ginger Paste (page 231)

1 fresh medium hot chili pepper, such as serrano or Fresno

Handful fresh cilantro

2 tablespoons extra-virgin olive oil

1 teaspoon ground coriander

1 teaspoon ground cumin

Fine sea salt

2 tablespoons all-purpose flour

16 wheat egg roll wrappers, plus extra in case any tear

Neutral oil, such as avocado or peanut oil, for frying

Lime wedges, for serving

1   Drain and rinse the lentils. Finely dice the onion. Thinly slice the green onions. Grate the garlic. Finely mince the chili pepper (remove the seeds for a milder flavor). Finely chop the cilantro (leaves and stems). Set aside.

2   Set a medium frying pan over medium heat. Once hot (sprinkle a few drops of water into the pan—the water should sizzle and evaporate quickly), pour the oil into the pan, then add the onion and cook, frequently stirring until softened, 5 to 7 minutes. Add the green onions, garlic, chili pepper, coriander, and cumin, and cook for 1 to 2 minutes until fragrant. Stir in the lentils and cilantro, and season with salt to taste.

3   Mix the flour with 3 tablespoons water to create a flour paste. Cut the egg roll wrappers in half diagonally and keep them covered to prevent them from drying out. To make the samosas, place half an egg roll wrapper on a cutting board with the point facing upward. Fold the left and right corners toward the middle to create a cone shape. Use the flour paste to close the sides.

4   Spoon in 1 rounded tablespoon of the lentil filling and fold over the top flap to close, using the flour paste as glue to seal it closed. Check that the samosa has no gaps or it will leak during frying.

5   Fill a heavy-bottom pan with 1 inch of neutral oil and heat over medium-high heat. Line a plate with paper towels and place it beside the stove. Once the oil reaches 350°F (180°C), work in batches to fry the samosas. Cook, turning every 30 seconds, until they are a light golden-brown color, about 2 minutes.

6   Drain on the paper towel–lined plate, and serve warm with lime wedges.

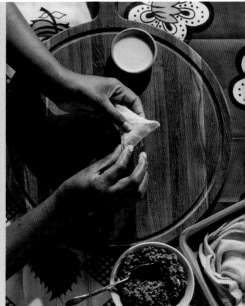

Makes about

16

samosas

feta & herb samosas

Samosas are incredibly common in Kenyan cuisine. So common that they sell them in gas stations, which has always surprised me because they usually call for a fair amount of work; making the filling, folding, and frying. These quick-fix samosas are made with a no-cook filling of feta and lots of herbs. They are best eaten immediately after frying when the cheese is soft and gooey!

8 ounces sheep feta cheese

1 to 2 large eggs

Large handful fresh cilantro

Large handful fresh parsley

Handful fresh mint

1 teaspoon coriander seeds

1 teaspoon dried oregano

1 tablespoon all-purpose flour

16 wheat egg roll wrappers, plus extra in case any tear

Neutral oil, such as avocado or peanut oil, for frying

Lime wedges, for serving

1   Crumble the feta cheese into a small bowl. Lightly beat 1 egg and add it to the bowl; the egg helps bind everything together, making it easier to work with. Some feta is crumbly and dry, so you may need 2 eggs. Discard the stems from the cilantro, parsley, and mint, so you have around 1½ ounces of herb leaves. Roughly chop the leaves and add to the bowl. Use a mortar and pestle or rolling pin to roughly crush the coriander seeds and add to the same bowl along with the oregano, mixing to fully combine.

2   In another bowl, combine the flour with 1 tablespoon water, and mix until it makes a runny but thick paste, similar to glue.

3   Cut the egg roll wrappers in half going from corner to corner, so each square becomes two triangles. Keep them covered with a damp paper towel to prevent them from drying out while making the samosas.

4   **To make the samosas:** Place one of the egg roll triangles on a cutting board with the central point facing upward. Fold the left and right corners toward the middle to create a cone shape. Dab a finger in the flour paste and run it along the sides like glue to close them, so there is only one central opening.

(recipe continues)

5   Use your hands to sprinkle in around 1 tablespoon of the feta filling into the opening, fold over the top flap to close, and use the flour paste to seal it. Check that the samosa has no gaps or it will leak when fried.

6   Fill a heavy-bottom pan with 1 inch of neutral oil and heat over medium-high heat. Line a plate with paper towels and place it beside the stove. Once the oil reaches 350°F (180°C), work in batches to fry the samosas. Cook, turning every 30 seconds, until they are a light golden-brown color, about 2 minutes.

7   Drain on the paper towel–lined plate.

8   Serve warm with lime wedges.

cherry tomato kachumbari

Typically prepared as a condiment, this refreshing and spicy salsa is one of the most common accompaniments to roasted or grilled meat in Kenyan cuisine and the surrounding countries. Most commonly made with a Roma tomato, the variations are infinite, each best suited to a particular dish. The key to a good kachumbari is cutting the vegetables very thinly. You can slice or dice, depending on what you are serving it with.

1 pint cherry tomatoes

½ small red onion

1 fresh medium hot chili pepper, such as serrano or Fresno

Small handful fresh cilantro

Fine sea salt

Juice of 1 lime or ½ large lemon

Slice the tomatoes into small circles. Cut the onion and chili pepper into small rings or finely dice. Discard the stems and roughly chop the cilantro leaves. Transfer the tomatoes, onion, and chili pepper to a serving bowl and season generously with salt. Squeeze over the lime juice, toss together, and set aside until ready to serve.

broccolini with gingery peas

I find that when cooking veggies, it feels more like a "main dish" when two vegetables come together. When I was a baby, my mom used to scatter peas on my eating tray, and I have never stopped eating them. The natural sweetness of the peas is a lovely complement to the slightly charred broccolini. If you make this dish with broccoli, trim the thicker stems and cut them into more manageable pieces.

2 bundles (roughly 12 ounces) broccolini

1-inch piece fresh ginger

Handful fresh herbs, such as mint, cilantro, parsley, or dill

3 tablespoons extra-virgin olive oil, divided

2 cups frozen peas

Fine sea salt

Freshly ground black pepper

1 teaspoon Aleppo chili pepper flakes, plus more for garnish

1   Trim the base stem off the broccolini. Peel and slice the ginger into very fine matchsticks. Discard the stems from the fresh herbs and roughly chop the leaves. Set everything aside.

2   Place a medium-size pan over medium-high heat. Once hot (sprinkle a few drops of water into the pan—the water should sizzle and evaporate quickly), pour 2 tablespoons of oil and ⅓ cup water into the pan. Arrange the broccolini into a single layer, bring to a boil, cover, and cook until all the water is gone. Once you hear the broccolini sizzling in the oil, remove the lid. Allow the broccolini

to char slightly on all sides; this may take 2 to 3 minutes for smaller broccolini, or about 7 minutes for larger pieces.

3   Lower the heat to medium. Add the remaining 1 tablespoon of oil, the ginger, peas, and the chili pepper flakes. Cook until the peas are no longer frozen but remain a bright green, 2 to 3 minutes.

4   Turn off the heat, stir in the herbs, then season generously with salt and black pepper. Garnish with Aleppo chili pepper flakes and serve warm.

koko's cabbage

My maternal grandmother, known as Koko to her grandchildren, always has a few heads of cabbage in her larder. Though they sell pre-sliced cabbage in the markets, she always insists on cutting it herself.

Before her home had a standing kitchen, all her meals were made on a traditional firewood stove, where she sat on a short stool just a foot off the ground to prepare all the meals for her eleven children and her young grandchildren. There were no countertops or cutting boards. So, with cabbage in one hand and a knife in the other, she would run her blade across the halved cabbage head, carefully shaving the thinnest slices. The style of how this cabbage is cooked is exemplary of traditional inland Kenyan cuisine: simple preparation with simple ingredients.

1 small green cabbage or
  ½ medium cabbage

2 medium carrots

Handful fresh cilantro

1 teaspoon fine sea salt

1 small red onion

2 tablespoons extra-virgin
  olive oil

Chapati (see pages 64 and
  68), grains, or any cooked
  protein, for serving

1 Cut the cabbage in half through the stem. Using a knife to follow along the natural V shape, cut out the hard stem. Place the cabbage cut side down on the cutting board, and cut into slices as thin as possible. Grate the carrots with the larger holes on a box grater. Finely chop the cilantro (leaves and stems). Combine the cabbage, carrots, and cilantro in a large mixing bowl. Add ½ teaspoon of salt and mix well. Taste before adding the rest of the salt, and mix again to season the vegetables evenly. Dice the onion.

2 Set a wide pan over medium heat. Once hot, place the oil in the pan, then add the onion and cook, stirring frequently with a wooden spoon to stop any burning, until the onion starts browning on the edges, 3 to 5 minutes. Add the cabbage mixture and stir well. Cover with a lid and cook until the cabbage reduces in volume and is no longer crunchy, about 5 minutes.

3 Uncover and cook off any remaining water. Serve warm with the chapati, grains, or any cooked protein.

sukuma wiki

The translation of sukuma wiki *is deceitful. In Swahili,* sukuma *means "to push" and* wiki *"the week," as in the day of the week. The name of this dish has nothing to do with energy, but rather it is a commentary on how cheap this dish is to prepare; cheap enough to push you through the week until you get paid.*

In Kenya, sukuma leaves can be purchased whole or precut. The market vendors cut them thin, even thinner than angel hair pasta. They grip the tightly bound bundles as they gently shave off layers with a steady hand that rivals a good barber. Sukuma can be your main dish or a side as part of a larger meal. A classic way to enjoy this is with ugali, cooked white cornmeal similar to firm grits or polenta.

1 pound collard greens

4 garlic cloves

2 medium tomatoes

1 thumb fresh ginger

3 tablespoons extra-virgin olive oil

Fine sea salt

1 Remove the thick stalks from the center of the collard green leaves. Arrange them in a neat stack, then roll the leaves into a tight cylinder. Gripping the bundle tight in one hand, use a sharp knife to finely slice the greens ¼-inch (1 cm) thick, being careful not to shred too thin or they will clump together when cooked.

2 Thinly slice the garlic. Dice the tomatoes. Peel and cut the ginger into small matchsticks.

3 Heat a shallow and wide pan over medium heat. Once hot, place the oil in the pan, then add the ginger and garlic, and cook until they are lightly brown on the edges, about 5 minutes. Add in the greens and mix to combine.

4 When the collards brighten in color to a vibrant green, add in the tomatoes, and cover with a lid to steam the mixture. When the greens have darkened in color and cooked down slightly, 2 to 3 minutes, remove the lid and season with salt to taste. Serve immediately.

zucchini & feta bhajias

I was living in London when I first learned that Kenya grew zucchini. I was grocery shopping when I picked up a package of zucchini (labeled as courgette) that read "grown in Kenya." This confused me because I have been spending my summers in Kenya since kindergarten, and never once had I seen a zucchini.

Kenya's agricultural industry had two markets at the time: food grown for locals and food grown for export. Since then, times have changed, and now the zucchini that was once exclusive to Europe has found its way into local supermarkets and slowly onto the menus of modern restaurants.

1 pound green zucchini

Fine sea salt

2 teaspoons coriander seeds

1 fresh medium hot chili pepper, such as serrano or Fresno

Handful fresh parsley

Handful fresh cilantro

4 ounces feta cheese

1 large egg

6 tablespoons chickpea flour

1 tablespoon Garlic Ginger Paste (page 231)

Neutral oil, such as avocado or peanut oil, for frying

Sea salt flakes

Herby Yogurt (page 226), for serving

1 Line a mixing bowl with a cheesecloth or a clean, thin kitchen towel. Cut the zucchini into matchsticks and place them in the lined bowl. Generously add fine sea salt, then set aside for 15 minutes to draw out any liquid.

2 After the zucchini has rested, gather the corners of the cloth so all the zucchini is at the bottom, and twist the excess fabric until you have a tight ball. Discard any liquid in the bowl. Over the sink, squeeze the zucchini ball, so the excess water comes out. Any water will make these soggy, so try to remove as much as you can. Place the zucchini back into the mixing bowl.

3 With a mortar and pestle or rolling pin, roughly crush the coriander seeds. Finely chop the chili pepper (remove the seeds for a milder flavor), parsley, and cilantro (leaves and stems). Crumble the feta. In a small bowl, lightly beat the egg. Add everything to the mixing bowl along with the chickpea flour, garlic ginger paste, and 1 teaspoon fine sea salt.

4 Use your hands to mix well until everything is evenly combined.

5 Fill a pan with ½ inch oil and heat to 350°F (180°C). Set a paper towel–lined plate beside the stove. When the oil is ready, working in batches, fry the fritters. With a metal dinner spoon, drop the batter into the hot oil, and use the back of the spoon to press them flat. Be sure to leave space between each fritter. Once the bottom has lightly browned, about 1 minute, use a fork or spatula to carefully flip each fritter and cook the other side until golden brown, another 1 to 2 minutes. Remove

from the oil, drain on the paper towel–lined plate, and immediately season with sea salt flakes.

6 Enjoy as a snack with the herby yogurt for dipping.

tip
These bhajias are great for brunch like a bhajia benedict, with poached eggs and herby yogurt drizzled on top.

chili cheese pommes anna

A delightful break from roast potatoes, pommes Anna is the less saucy version of a gratin. Thinly sliced potatoes tossed in butter are layered into a skillet and cooked until the exterior is crisp. The layers are perfect for sneaking in some added flavor. Feta and goat cheese work well, adding creaminess to the buttery potatoes without adding more oil.

1½ pounds russet potatoes

4 green onions

1 fresh medium hot chili pepper (serrano or Fresno)

Small handful fresh cilantro

3½ ounces feta or soft goat's cheese

4 garlic cloves

4 tablespoons unsalted butter

Fine sea salt

1   Preheat the oven to 400°F (200°C) and arrange a rack on the middle shelf of the oven. Cut out a piece of parchment paper the same size as the top rim of a 12-inch, oven-safe frying pan.

2   Peel the potatoes and use a mandolin or a knife to thinly slice them. Place in a large mixing bowl and set aside.

3   Finely chop the green onions, chili (remove the seeds for a milder flavor), and cilantro (leaves and stems), and place in a separate bowl. Crumble in the feta cheese and mix well. Set aside.

4   Thinly slice the garlic. Melt the butter in the frying pan set over medium heat. Once the butter has melted, add the garlic and cook, stirring, until fragrant, 1 to 2 minutes. Pour the garlicky butter over the potatoes. Season well

with a few pinches of salt and use a spatula to combine everything.

5   Using the same frying pan, carefully arrange one-third of the potatoes in layers, ensuring each layer is flat. Sprinkle with half of the cheese mixture. Add another layer of potatoes and sprinkle with the remaining cheese mixture. Finish with a final potato layer and cover with the cut piece of parchment.

6   Cook the potatoes on the stove over medium-high heat until the bottom begins to sizzle and lightly browns, about 5 minutes. Finish cooking in the oven. After 15 minutes, remove the parchment to allow the top to brown, another 15 to 20 minutes. Flip onto a wide platter, being careful as the pan is hot. Serve with a small knife so people can cut their own slice.

mukimo croquettes

Mukimo (also called irio) is a green mashed potato dish with its color taken from leafy greens. Inspired by that dish, my version uses spinach for an almost cartoonlike green hue. For a more traditional Kenyan version, add 1 cup of cooked maize, though it's an ingredient I've never cared for, so I leave it out of mine. Instead, I use peas to add a similar sweetness.

For the Croquettes

1 pound gold potatoes

Fine sea salt

2 garlic cloves

2 tablespoons extra-virgin olive oil

1 teaspoon smoked paprika

3 tightly packed cups (6 ounces) spinach leaves

Freshly ground black pepper

1 cup thawed frozen peas

2 large eggs

½ cup all-purpose flour

1 cup plain breadcrumbs

Neutral oil, such as avocado or peanut oil, for frying

Sea salt flakes

For the Sauce

1 garlic clove

2 tablespoons mayonnaise

1 tablespoon Dijon mustard

1 tablespoon extra-virgin olive oil

¼ teaspoon sea salt

1   **Cook the potatoes:** Peel and dice the potatoes into 1-inch chunks. Place the potatoes into a large pot and fill with water to cover by 1 inch, then generously add sea salt. Bring to a boil and cook until the potatoes feel tender when pricked with a fork, about 15 minutes.

2   **Make the sauce:** While the potatoes are boiling, prepare the sauce. In a small bowl, using a Microplane, grate the garlic. Stir in the mayonnaise, Dijon mustard, olive oil, and salt. Mix until smooth, then set aside until ready to serve.

3   **Prepare the croquettes:** When the potatoes are ready, drain the potatoes, then mash them or put through a ricer for a smoother consistency. Set aside.

4   Thinly slice the garlic. Set a medium-size skillet over medium-low heat. Once hot, pour the olive oil into the pan, then add the garlic and paprika and cook, stirring frequently, until fragrant but not burnt, about 1 minute.

5   Add the spinach, and season well with sea salt and black pepper. Mix everything to combine and cook until the spinach has fully wilted, 3 to 5 minutes. Transfer the mixture to a small food processor and puree until smooth.

6   Mix the mashed potato with the spinach puree and peas. Adjust the salt and pepper to taste if needed.

7   Prepare a baking sheet lined with parchment paper for easy cleanup.

8   Lightly beat the eggs in a bowl. In two
    separate bowls, add the flour and the
    breadcrumbs. With well-floured hands, shape
    the potato mixture into 2-inch-long sticks
    (about 2 tablespoons each) and then roll
    each of the croquette sticks in the flour until
    well coated. Set aside each croquette on the
    baking sheet.

9   Using a fork and working one at a time, roll
    each croquette in the egg until fully coated,
    then roll in the breadcrumbs. Repeat, coating
    each croquette twice in the egg and then the
    breadcrumbs, then set aside on the baking

    sheet until each croquette is fully coated. Let
    sit for 10 minutes before frying.

10 Heat a heavy-bottom pan on medium-
    high heat with 1 inch neutral oil until the
    temperature reaches 350°F (180°C). While the
    oil heats, line a plate with paper towels and
    place beside the stove. In batches, add the
    croquettes and fry until golden brown, turning
    as needed with a fork so all sides are evenly
    browned, 2 to 3 minutes on each side. Drain on
    the paper towel–lined plate and season with
    sea salt flakes. Transfer to a serving platter
    and serve warm with the sauce on the side.

Serves

6

roasted sweet potato with chili & lime

On the Kenyan coast, street food vendors have charcoal grills roasting a variety of vegetables all day long. The sweet potatoes are cooked skin-on, and when ordered, the vendors split them open before adding a generous squeeze of lime and a few shakes of chili salt. Feel free to throw these on the grill when possible, but the seasoning alone will liven up otherwise boring roasted sweet potatoes.

3 pounds sweet potatoes

2 tablespoons extra-virgin olive oil

Fine sea salt

1 lime

1 teaspoon Aleppo chili pepper flakes, plus more for garnish

1 teaspoon dried urfa chili or smoked paprika

¼ teaspoon cayenne pepper

1   Position a rack in the center of your oven, and preheat to 425°F (220°C). Line a baking tray with parchment paper or foil.

2   Arrange the sweet potatoes on the prepared tray. Using a fork or paring knife, prick them a few times each, then toss with the oil and 1 teaspoon salt. Roast until they are fork-tender and lightly browned, 45 to 50 minutes.

3   Zest the lime into a small bowl, and cut the lime into wedges. Add the chili pepper flakes, urfa chili, cayenne pepper, and salt to taste to the bowl of lime zest. Mix well to combine.

4   Transfer the cooked sweet potatoes to a serving platter. Squeeze the lime wedges over the sweet potatoes. Garnish with the lime zest and an extra sprinkle of chili pepper flakes.

veggies

57

flatbreads,

rice

&

friends

If there is a dish that can attest to one's culinary skills, it is chapati! The best chapati is soft with a slight chew and many flaky layers. This unleavened flatbread is a staple in Kenyan cuisine, as well as in neighboring countries. Despite sharing a name with the Indian bread, it's better likened to a paratha due to its layered structure.

The key to successfully making chapati is practice and time. Every family knows who the excellent chapati makers are and who isn't allowed to touch them.

Chapati making is commonly a communal affair, made in an assembly line with each cook preparing a step. The typical ingredients are simple: flour, water, salt, and fat. The dough is prepared in a basin, starting with the flour and salt. Room-temperature water is slowly streamed in as it's mixed by hand. Determining the correct amount of water is critical here. Add too little, and the chapati will be rock hard and double as a frisbee once cooked. Too much water and they won't hold their shape. This makes preparing the dough the most critical step in chapati making, and the role is naturally left to the best cook.

Once the base dough is made, it's divided and shaped into balls, and the assembly line begins; the jobs include rolling, adding the fat, final shaping, and cooking. One person can accomplish these tasks, but cooking communally serves a dual function of making the process more leisurely and giving people time to socialize.

My grandmother's kitchen has always been loud, filled with constant storytelling as she and the neighbors cooked together. Old Maasai ladies speak so loudly! I think it's a defense mechanism to ward off unwanted visitors or disruptions as they enjoy one another's company while preparing food.

At family gatherings in California, chapati is always present and often left to be made until the last minute so that enough free laborers are present to chip in. I've adopted a similar philosophy in the dinners I host for friends. The slower, long-cooking dishes will be prepared ahead of time, and I'll leave the laborious tasks like preparing chapatis or samosas to be completed once a few guests have arrived.

This, I've come to learn, contrasts with a typical American dinner party where the host does all the work before the guests arrive. I have always found these dinner parties to be brief and a bit boring. I grew up in homes where cooking together was the bulk of the party, and the conclusion was the dinner. There was a time in American history (and currently for some) when dinner parties were used as a status symbol to show off to friends. I invite people to dinner because I wish to spend time with them. So, I shamelessly put my friends to work as we huddle in the kitchen, enjoying one another's company while preparing a meal.

garlic butter chapati

The women in my family all have their secrets to making the perfect tender, flaky chapati. Everyone follows the Maasai style of dough that uses both water and milk. My grandmother loves a soft chapati, so she avoids using too much fat, as it makes the flatbread crispy as it cooks. My aunt Tilly likes to add a spoonful of sugar to achieve a softer dough. My recipe pulls in the best tips from my family, but there are times where more fat can be better, and that time is when butter is involved!

4 cups (520 grams) unbleached all-purpose flour, plus additional for rolling

3 teaspoons fine sea salt

1 tablespoon sugar

1 cup warm milk

⅓ cup extra-virgin olive oil

½ cup lukewarm water

Handful fresh cilantro or parsley

4 garlic cloves

4 tablespoons melted unsalted butter

1   In a large bowl, mix the flour, 2 teaspoons of salt, and the sugar. While continuously stirring, slowly pour in the milk. Once the milk is fully mixed in, add 2 tablespoons of oil, keep stirring, and add just enough of the lukewarm water until it becomes a scraggly dough. Start to knead the dough, adding small splashes of water until there are no more dry spots. Note, you may not use all the water.

2   Turn the dough onto a clean, lightly floured surface and knead until the dough comes together and is elastic and smooth, 3 to 5 minutes. Pat the dough into a rectangle. Lightly brush the surface of the dough with oil before covering with plastic wrap or a clean kitchen towel and allow it to rest for about 15 minutes. The dough has rested long enough when it has softened in texture.

3   While the dough is resting, prepare the garlic butter. Discard the stems and finely chop the cilantro leaves. Grate the garlic. Mix the

melted butter with the herbs and garlic in a small bowl, and set aside.

4   Use a rolling pin to roll out the dough into a thin rectangle that's at least 18 x 24-inches, but feel free to go thinner. It's okay if there are a few small tears. If the dough springs back when rolled, it needs to rest longer.

5   Using a pastry brush, coat the surface of the rolled out dough with the garlic butter. Lightly sprinkle 1 tablespoon flour on top. Starting from the bottom edge, roll the dough upward into itself until it forms a log shape. Cut the dough into 8 even pieces. Press the dough pieces cut side up into small circles. Cover and let rest for 30 minutes.

6   Lightly dust a work surface and a rolling pin. While working with a dough piece, keep the rest of the dough pieces covered so they don't dry out.

(recipe continues)

tips

If you're a garlic butter lover, double up! Use half in the chapati and brush on the rest on the hot chapati right when it comes off the stove.

Level up your chapati!

All-purpose flour is great for learning. Classic chapati is made with a fine wheat flour called atta mark 1. This gives a chewier bread texture, but if you use this type of flour, you may need more water when making your base dough and increase the dough rest times.

Storage & Reheating

Store in a zip-top plastic bag at room temperature for up to 2 days. Gently warm in a dry pan on low heat until they become gently flexible.

7   Working with one piece at a time, place the dough cut side facing up. Roll the dough into a 9- to 10-inch disc, frequently rotating to help maintain its shape. If the dough springs back when rolled, it needs to rest longer.

8   Heat a nonstick frying pan over medium-high heat. Once hot (sprinkle a few drops of water into the pan—the water should sizzle and evaporate quickly), lightly brush with oil, and carefully lay down the rolled out dough. Once the dough is no longer sticky on the surface, about 1 minute, lightly brush with oil, flip, and cook the other side for another 30 seconds to 1 minute until golden brown, lightly brushing the top with oil. It's a good sign if the chapati puffs up and bubbles! Repeat with the remaining dough, stacking the cooked chapatis on a plate. Keep covered until ready to serve.

pumpkin chapati

This staple flatbread is commonly made with flour, oil, salt, and water. However, in some areas of Kenya, mashed vegetables such as pumpkin or squash are also popular additions. Pumpkin chapatis are incredibly tender due to the added moisture.

**2 cups (260 grams)
unbleached all-purpose flour**

1½ teaspoons fine sea salt

**1 cup (215 grams) canned
pumpkin puree**

**6 tablespoons melted unsalted
butter**

1 Use your hands to mix the flour and salt in a large mixing bowl. Make a well in the center, add the pumpkin puree and 1 tablespoon of melted butter, and mix until fully combined and a loose dough forms.

2 Once the dough begins to pull together, turn it onto a cleaned and lightly floured surface and knead. Continue to knead the dough until smooth, about 5 minutes. Cover with plastic wrap or a clean kitchen towel and let it rest until the dough relaxes, about 15 minutes. If the dough feels too springy, it needs to rest for longer.

3 Roll out the dough on a lightly floured surface until it's thin. Don't worry if the dough tears. If the dough is shrinking as you roll, cover it to allow it to rest for another 10 minutes.

4 Once the dough is stretched thin, brush the entire surface with the melted butter. Lightly sprinkle a few pinches of flour on top of the butter. Working from the edge nearest you, roll the dough into a log. Cut into 6 pieces.

5 When ready to cook, heat a wide nonstick frying pan over medium-high. While the pan is heating, roll out the dough. Keep the rest of the pieces covered with a clean kitchen towel to prevent them from drying out.

6 To begin rolling, first lightly flour your hands and a rolling pin. With the cut side facing up, press down the chapati piece into a flat disc.

7 Working with one piece at a time, place the dough cut side facing up. Roll the dough into an 8- to 9-inch disc, frequently rotating to help maintain its circular shape. If the dough springs back when rolled, it needs to rest longer.

8 Once the pan is hot (sprinkle a few drops of water into the pan—the water should sizzle and evaporate quickly), lightly brush with the melted butter, and carefully lay down the rolled-out dough. Once the dough is no longer sticky on the surface, about 1 minute, lightly brush the top with butter, flip, and cook the other side for another 30 seconds to 1 minute until golden brown, lightly brushing the top with butter. It's a good sign if the chapati puffs up and bubbles! Repeat with the remaining dough, stacking the cooked chapatis on a plate. Keep covered until ready to serve.

**Storage &
Reheating:**

Store in a zip-top plastic bag at room temperature for up to 2 days. Gently warm in a dry pan on low heat until they become gently flexible.

herby fluffy flatbread

This is one of those recipes that's nice to have in your back pocket. It's for all those occasions when something I want to cook needs a bread accompaniment, but I don't have any. I make this primarily for brunch when I want a tomato-y egg dish but need something to scoop it up.

2 springs fresh rosemary or oregano (or 2 teaspoons dried)

Handful fresh parsley (optional)

1½ cups (195 grams) all-purpose flour, plus extra for kneading

1 cup whole-fat yogurt

1½ teaspoons baking powder

1 teaspoon fine sea salt

1 Discard the stems and finely chop the rosemary and parsley. In a mixing bowl, using a wooden spoon, combine the flour, rosemary, parsley, yogurt, baking powder, and salt until a dough forms.

2 Lightly dust a clean work surface with flour and knead the dough until smooth. Divide the dough into 6 even pieces. Shape each piece into a smooth ball and roll out each ball until it is roughly ¼-inch thick.

3 Heat a skillet over medium-high heat. Once hot (sprinkle a few drops of water into the pan—the water should sizzle and evaporate quickly), cook each piece of bread in the dry skillet for 2 to 3 minutes on each side; the bread should puff up as it cooks and be lightly browned when finished. Enjoy the day you make them for the freshest bread.

couscous

I didn't start cooking couscous until college when my friend Baye was preparing some Senegalese yassa poulet, aka chicken with lemony onions, with a side of couscous. The preparation of the couscous was so simple; for that fact alone, I have always made a point to have it on hand should I need to make a starch in a pinch. Depending on what dish it accompanies, you can add loads of toppings to your couscous.

Moroccan couscous (not pearls)

Fine sea salt

Bring a pot or kettle of water to a boil over high heat. Place your desired quantity of couscous in a bowl and mix in a few pinches of salt. Pour the hot water over the couscous until it is submerged by ½ inch, then cover it with a plate and let it steam for 5 minutes. Uncover and fluff with a fork before serving.

Topping suggestions

Topping suggestions: raisins, sliced hard-boiled egg, extra-virgin olive oil, green onions, olives, sauteed onions, feta cheese.

jeera & garlic rice

Serves **2** to **4** as a side

I try to avoid serving just plain white rice whenever possible. My family always has to add something to the rice, even a cup of frozen peas.

The flavor in the jeera (aka cumin seeds) wakes up when sizzled in the hot butter. Plenty of garlic is used as the flavor becomes mild as it steams with the rice.

1¼ cups basmati rice

6 garlic cloves

2 tablespoons unsalted butter, ghee, or extra-virgin olive oil

1 teaspoon cumin seeds

1 teaspoon fine sea salt

1 cup frozen peas or mixed vegetables (optional)

1 In a fine mesh strainer or a large bowl, wash the rice under cold water until the water runs nearly clear. This step may need to be repeated two or more times until the water is mostly clear.

2 Finely mince the garlic. Set a medium-size pot over medium-low heat. Once hot, melt the butter. Once melted, add the garlic and cumin seeds and season with ½ teaspoon of salt. Cook, stirring constantly to prevent burning, until the garlic is fragrant and slightly starting to color, 1 to 2 minutes.

3 Add the washed rice and stir in the frozen peas (if using), along with 1½ cups water and the remaining ½ teaspoon of salt. Increase the heat to high. Once at a boil, stir the rice, lower the heat to medium-low, cover, and cook until all the water has been absorbed, 10 to 12 minutes. Remove from the heat and leave covered for another 5 minutes. Uncover and fluff with a fork before serving.

jollof rice

Jollof is the most famous West African dish. Originally hailing from Senegambia, each West African nation has its interpretation of the dish. The foundation of the dish is rice cooked in a tomato-based stew. A signature of Nigerian jollof is the addition of red peppers. Nigerian party jollof typically has a smoky finish, but I prefer the stew flavors to shine through, so this recipe is finished in the oven. For many people, jollof is arguably a main dish, but I prefer to serve it alongside a roasted or stewed protein.

tip

If you don't have foil, use parchment paper. Sealing the pot this way is essential for properly steaming the rice.

2 cups basmati rice

2 medium red bell peppers

2 small to medium red onions

1 (14-ounce) can diced tomatoes

1 tablespoon Garlic Ginger Paste (page 231)

1 fresh very hot chili pepper, such as habanero or Scotch bonnet

⅓ cup oil (50:50 avocado oil and palm oil, or all avocado oil)

Few sprigs fresh thyme or ½ teaspoon dried thyme

2½ cups chicken or vegetable stock

2 teaspoons Curry Powder (page 239)

2 teaspoons paprika

Fine sea salt

1   Preheat the oven to 350°F (180°C) and place the rack on the bottom shelf.

2   In a fine mesh strainer or a large bowl, wash the rice under cold water until the water runs nearly clear. This step may need to be repeated two or more times until the water is mostly clear.

3   Roughly chop the bell peppers and onions. Add the tomatoes with their liquid to a blender, then add the bell peppers, onions, garlic ginger paste, and chili pepper (remove the seeds for a milder flavor) and puree until smooth.

4   Pour the stew base into a braising pot with a fitted lid. Cook uncovered over medium

heat, occasionally stirring, until the water has cooked off, 15 to 20 minutes.

5   Add the oil and "fry" the sauce until it has thickened and slightly darkened in color, 5 to 10 minutes. The stew is ready when the tomatoes have sweetened and the stew is no longer runny.

6   Pick off the leaves from the thyme sprig and discard the stems. Stir in the thyme leaves, chicken stock, curry powder, and paprika. Bring to a simmer and season with salt to taste. Stir in the washed rice, seal tightly with foil, cover with the pot lid, and bake for 25 minutes. Remove from the oven and leave to steam for 10 minutes. Uncover and fluff the rice with a fork before serving.

golden chicken & "rice"

Though it's the shape of rice, orzo is indeed a pasta. As someone who grew up with parents from two rice-loving cultures, orzo is a welcome break as it almost seamlessly works in many meals where I typically would have prepared rice. In this recipe, the orzo replaces basmati rice in a chicken-pilau-inspired recipe. Pilau is an East African one-pot dish where rice is cooked with braised meat and stock. Because orzo is pasta, the bottom of the pot can get a bit sticky, but prepared in a pan with the right amount of slip, you'll have a lovely crunchy treat at the bottom.

8 boneless skinless chicken thighs

3 teaspoons Butcher's Masala (page 238), divided

1 teaspoon fine sea salt

1 cup cherry tomatoes

4 medium green onions

1 fresh medium hot chili pepper, such as serrano or Fresno

Small handful fresh cilantro

3 tablespoons extra-virgin olive oil, plus more as needed

1 tablespoon Garlic Ginger Paste (page 231)

1 teaspoon ground turmeric

1 pound orzo pasta

2½ cups chicken stock

1 Season the chicken thighs with 2 teaspoons of butcher's masala and the salt. Set aside.

2 Halve the tomatoes, thinly slice the green onions and chili pepper (remove the seeds for a milder flavor), and finely chop the cilantro. Set aside.

3 Heat a wide nonstick pan over medium-high heat. Once hot, pour the oil into the pan. Carefully place the chicken thighs in the pan in a single layer, and cook until browned, 3 to 4 minutes on each side; they do not need to be fully cooked through. Place the browned chicken on a plate to rest.

4 To the same pan, combine the green onions, chili, cilantro, garlic ginger paste, remaining 1 teaspoon of butcher's masala, and the

turmeric. If the pan looks dry, add an extra lug of oil. Once aromatic, stir in the orzo and lightly toast.

5 Lower the heat to medium. Stir in the tomatoes and chicken stock, using a wooden cooking spoon to scrape the bottom well. Place the chicken thighs on top and cook covered, 10 to 12 minutes, occasionally stirring to keep the orzo from sticking to the bottom. The dish will be ready to serve when the orzo has absorbed all the liquid.

6 Serve straight out of the pan and enjoy the crisped-up pieces of orzo stuck to the bottom.

kijani seafood pilau

Pilau is an all-in-one rice dish. You'll find different versions across East Africa, each with their own combinations of meat and vegetables cooked with a long-grain rice. This pilau is more about aromatics; the rice is cooked in a veggie-packed base that gives it a vibrant green (aka kijani) color, and it's then topped with fresh seafood. The shellfish adds fragrance to the rice as the steaming process releases their natural brine.

¼ pound calamari tubes and tentacles

1 pound peeled and deveined shrimp

Fine sea salt

Handful fresh cilantro

8 medium green onions

1 fresh medium hot chili pepper, such as serrano or Fresno

1 (5-ounce) bag baby spinach

2 cups stock, such as shellfish or vegetable

½ medium yellow onion

3 tablespoons extra-virgin olive oil

1 tablespoon plus 1 teaspoon Garlic Ginger Paste (page 231)

1¼ cups basmati rice

2 teaspoons Curry Powder (page 239)

1 cup frozen peas

½ pound mussels or clams

1   Cut the calamari tubes into ½-inch rounds. To a large bowl, add the rounds, tentacles, and shrimp and season with salt. Set aside.

2   Roughly chop the cilantro (leaves and stems), green onions, and chili pepper (remove the seeds for a milder flavor), and add to a blender with the spinach and stock. Puree until smooth. Dice the yellow onion.

3   Heat a wide pan or braising dish over medium heat. Once hot, pour the oil into the pan, then add the onion and garlic ginger paste and cook, stirring, until the onion becomes translucent, 5 to 7 minutes. Stir in the rice and curry powder. Toast for about 2 minutes, then add the green puree. Mix well to combine.

4   Increase the heat to medium-high and boil for 5 minutes. Stir in the peas and carefully arrange the calamari, shrimp, and mussels on top. Lower the heat to medium-low, cover, and cook until the rice is tender, 12 to 15 minutes. If there's still a touch of liquid, turn off the heat and let the rice steam for 10 minutes. Remove the seafood from the pan and transfer the rice to a serving bowl. Arrange the seafood over the rice and serve immediately.

tip

Make your own stock! Buy shell-on shrimp and boil the shells with the green onion trimmings, onion peel, salt, and 2½ cups water for 5 minutes. Strain before use.

shrimp fried rice

Fried rice in West Africa is everywhere. Though it differs from Asian-style fried rice, the concept is more or less the same: a combination of protein and vegetables is prepared over high heat with cooked rice. Something I enjoy about Nigerian fried rice is the depth of flavor. The rice used isn't plain but instead cooked in stock. Curry powder adds fragrance to the dish and leaves behind a signature yellow tint.

tip
Fried rice is amazing for brunch, so feel free to throw a sunny-side up egg on top!

½ pound raw peeled and deveined small shrimp

2 teaspoons Curry Powder (page 239), divided

Juice of 1 lemon

Fine sea salt

1 medium carrot

8 medium green onions

3 tablespoons neutral oil, such as avocado or peanut oil

1 cup cooked or frozen mixed vegetables or trimmed French beans

1½ cups leftover cooked rice

2 tablespoons Garlic Ginger Paste (page 231)

Shito chili oil, for serving (optional)

1   In a medium-size bowl, season the shrimp with 1 teaspoon of curry powder, the lemon juice, and salt. Set aside. Peel and finely grate the carrot. Thinly slice the green onions.

2   Heat a wide frying pan or wok over medium-high heat. Once hot (sprinkle a few drops of water into the pan—the water should sizzle and evaporate quickly), pour the oil into the pan, then add the shrimp and cook, stirring occasionally, until they turn pink; the cook time will depend on the size of your shrimp.

Remove the shrimp from the pan and set aside.

3   Add the mixed vegetables to the same pan and cook, stirring occasionally, until lightly charred, 3 to 5 minutes. Add the carrot, rice, and garlic ginger paste, and using a wooden spoon, stir to separate the rice grains. Season with the remaining 1 teaspoon curry powder and salt and mix well to combine. Once the rice is toasted, after about 5 minutes, add the cooked shrimp and green onions and mix well. This is best served warm with shito chili oil.

swahili chicken biriyani

The cuisine of the Swahili coast is spectacular. Influenced by the Arab traders who settled there, alongside all those who have traded on the Indian Ocean, this has led to slightly differing dishes from their international counterparts. I love the Swahili version of biriyani because it is SAUCY! Instead of a mixed rice dish, a rich gravy with chunks of chicken cascades over colorfully fragrant basmati rice.

1 cup plain whole-milk yogurt

2 tablespoons Garlic Ginger Paste (page 231)

2 tablespoons Butcher's Masala (page 238)

Juice of 1 lemon

Fine sea salt

2 pounds boneless skinless chicken thighs

6 shallots or 1 medium red onion

2 fresh medium hot chili peppers, such as serrano or Fresno

4 medium tomatoes

Handful fresh cilantro

1 cup neutral oil, such as avocado or peanut oil

2 tablespoons tomato paste

2½ cups basmati rice

10 cardamom pods

Saffron or ground turmeric

1 Whisk together the yogurt, garlic ginger paste, butcher's masala, lemon juice, and 2 teaspoons salt. Cut the chicken into 2-inch chunks, toss in the marinade, and allow to sit for at least 30 minutes or overnight in the refrigerator.

2 Thinly slice the shallots and chili peppers (remove the seeds for a milder flavor). Dice the tomatoes. Roughly chop the cilantro (leaves and stems).

3 Fill a medium pot with 1 inch of oil and heat over medium-high heat. Prepare a plate lined with paper towels and set beside the stove. Once the oil is hot, add the shallots and cook, constantly stirring, until crispy and golden brown, 5 to 8 minutes. Using a slotted spoon, remove the shallots and place on the paper towel–lined plate to drain, seasoning with salt to taste. Reserve the oil in a heatproof container.

(recipe continues)

4   Heat ¼ cup of the reserved shallot oil in a
    wide braising dish or Dutch oven over medium
    heat. When the oil is shimmering, add the
    tomato paste and cook, stirring frequently,
    until darkened, 2 to 3 minutes. Add half
    the sliced chilis and all the diced tomatoes.
    Cover with a lid and cook until the tomatoes
    have broken down, 8 to 12 minutes. Add the
    marinated chicken and half the fried shallots.
    Cook, stirring occasionally, until the chicken
    has cooked and the sauce thickens, about
    20 minutes. If needed, remove the lid to let the
    sauce thicken further.

5   While the chicken is simmering, cook the rice.
    In a fine mesh strainer or a large bowl, wash
    the rice under cold water until the water runs
    nearly clear. This step may need to be repeated
    two or more times until the water is mostly
    clear. Transfer the washed and drained rice
    to a medium pot (you can use the same pot as
    the shallots). Add 3 cups water, the cardamom
    pods, and ½ teaspoon salt. Bring to a boil,
    then lower to a simmer, partially cover, and
    cook until all the water has been absorbed,
    12 to 15 minutes. Mix the saffron with
    2 tablespoons of hot water. Once the water has
    been absorbed by the rice, pour the saffron
    water over the top, cover, and let steam for
    10 minutes before fluffing with a fork.

6   To serve family style, create a base layer of
    rice on a large serving platter. Spoon the
    chicken into the center. Top with the reserved
    fried shallots and sliced chilis.

eggs, chicken & seafood

chicken & the egg

You'll find influences of British food woven into bits of African cuisine, predominantly due to colonialism, including pub culture. My appreciation for pubs grew when I lived in London. Pub grub is all about comfort, and Scotch eggs are one of my favorites. Seasoned sausage is wrapped around boiled eggs, covered with breadcrumbs, then deep-fried.

8 medium eggs, at room temperature, divided

Handful fresh parsley

Handful fresh cilantro

1 pound ground chicken

1 tablespoon extra-virgin olive oil

2½ teaspoons Butcher's Masala (page 238)

2 teaspoons fine sea salt

⅔ cup all-purpose flour

⅔ cup plain breadcrumbs

1 teaspoon coriander seeds

1 teaspoon nigella seeds or black sesame seeds

Neutral oil, such as avocado or peanut oil, for frying

1 Bring a large saucepan of water to a boil. Once the water is boiling, reduce the heat to low and use a slotted spoon to gently lower in 6 eggs. Cook for 7 minutes.

2 While the eggs cook, prepare an ice bath. Fill a medium bowl halfway with cold water and a good scoop of ice. Once the eggs are ready, using a slotted spoon, quickly place the eggs into the ice bath to immediately stop the cooking process. After 5 minutes, remove the eggs, peel them, and pat dry. Set aside.

3 Roughly chop the parsley and cilantro (leaves and stems). Mix the herbs, chicken, olive oil, butcher's masala, and salt in a bowl. Divide into six equal portions.

4 In separate shallow bowls, place the flour, the 2 remaining eggs, and the breadcrumbs. Season the eggs with salt and beat with a fork until combined.

5 Using a mortar and pestle or rolling pin, roughly crush the coriander seeds. Combine the coriander seeds and nigella seeds with the breadcrumbs.

6 Working with one boiled egg at a time, evenly coat the egg in the flour and shape one portion of the ground chicken around the egg.

7 Dip the chicken-encased egg back into the flour, then into the egg wash, and then into the breadcrumbs, coating evenly. Set aside on a plate and repeat with the remaining eggs.

8 In a large saucepan, heat 2 inches neutral oil to 350°F (180°C). Line a plate with paper towels and place beside the stove. Once the oil is hot, add the eggs and fry, 2 to 3 minutes, then flip and fry the other side until evenly browned, another 2 to 3 minutes. Remove the eggs from the oil with a slotted spoon and place on the paper towel–lined plate to absorb excess fat. Serve warm, cutting in half or in quarters to reveal that jammy egg yolk.

chips mayai

Chips, or fries, are everywhere in Kenya. They're a popular street food and a typical side dish at cafés. They are so popular that they've even found their way into breakfast! Cooked with scrambled eggs (mayai in Swahili) and various veggies and spices, this fried omelet is a popular street food in Tanzania. Still, it is beloved in all Swahili-speaking regions.

½ medium onion

½ medium green bell pepper

1 medium tomato

Extra-virgin olive oil

Fine sea salt

4 large eggs

½ teaspoon chili powder (Kashmiri preferred)

Small handful fresh cilantro

Neutral oil, such as avocado or peanut oil, for frying

½ pound waxy potatoes

2 tablespoons unsalted butter, divided

½ batch Cherry Tomato Kachumbari (page 39), for garnish

1   Slice the onion and dice the bell pepper and tomato. Heat a 10-inch nonstick frying pan over medium heat. Once hot, drizzle enough olive oil into the pan to coat the surface lightly, then add the sliced onion and cook, stirring occasionally, until it begins to soften, 4 to 5 minutes.

2   Add the bell pepper and tomato and cook, stirring frequently, until the tomatoes have released their liquid and the pepper has softened but is still a vibrant green, 4 to 6 minutes. Season well with salt and transfer to a medium-size mixing bowl. Set the frying pan aside to use again.

3   In the same bowl, add the eggs, chili powder, and a few pinches salt. Roughly chop the cilantro (leaves and stems) and add to the bowl. Whisk to combine and set aside.

4   Fill a separate medium-size pot with 2 inches neutral oil and heat to 350°F (180°C). While the oil heats, prepare a plate lined with paper towels and set beside the stove for later. Peel and cut the potatoes into ½-inch-thick sticks. Pat the potatoes dry using a clean kitchen

towel. In batches, fry the potato sticks in the oil, gently stirring to prevent sticking, until they're tender and lightly golden, 5 to 7 minutes. Drain the fries on the paper towel–lined plate and lightly season with salt to taste.

5   Set the 10-inch frying pan over medium-low heat and melt 1 tablespoon of butter. Once melted, pour in the egg mixture, and with a wooden spoon or spatula, scramble the eggs until halfway cooked. Spread into an even layer like an omelet, then press the fries onto the eggs. Gently shake the pan to keep the bottom from sticking.

6   Place a large plate (wider than the pan) face down on the frying pan. Using a kitchen towel to protect yourself, flip the omelet onto the plate with one swift motion.

7   Melt the remaining 1 tablespoon of butter in the pan, then slide the omelet back in, so the other side can cook until set, 2 to 3 minutes. Transfer to a serving platter, garnish with the cherry tomato kachumbari, and serve immediately.

mayai pasua

Classic mayai pasua can be found anywhere in Nairobi, Kenya. As an affordable street food to prepare, it consists of hard-boiled eggs (mayai) that are peeled and halved, then topped with a pile of kachumbari, which is a tomato salsa similar to Mexican pico de gallo. They get a generous squeeze of popular condiments such as tomato ketchup or chili sauce. I like to serve these as a "lazy" alternative to the American deviled eggs, cooking them with jammy yolks and topping them with kachumbari and a tangy Dijonnaise.

6 large eggs, room temperature

1 tablespoon Dijon mustard

1 tablespoon mayonnaise

Fine sea salt

½ batch finely diced Cherry Tomato Kachumbari (page 39)

1 Bring a pot of water to a boil. Reduce the heat to a simmer, and using a slotted spoon, carefully lower the eggs into the pot and cook for precisely 7 minutes. While the eggs are cooking, prepare an ice bath. Fill a medium bowl halfway with cold water and a good scoop of ice. When the eggs are ready, using a slotted spoon, immediately transfer them to the ice bath to immediately stop the cooking process. Peel when cool enough to handle.

2 In a separate small bowl, combine the mustard and mayonnaise.

3 When ready to serve, cut the eggs in half from top to bottom and place them on a serving platter with the yolk facing upward. Season with salt to taste, top with a drizzle of Dijonnaise, and add a heaping spoonful of cherry tomato kachumbari.

pili pili eggs

In any great hotel breakfast buffet, there's always an egg station. Across the African continent, I find that omelets aren't just beaten eggs that are then stuffed with a filling of your choice, but rather, the eggs are beaten with a combination of finely chopped fresh veggies so that it all cooks together. From Kenya to Ghana, I've regularly been served eggs beaten with tomato, onion, and chili peppers to start. Removing the pain of making individual omelets at home, I make a sharing pan of eggs, typically interchanging the onion and garlic depending on what I have on hand.

tip
Sprinkle on additional toppings such as feta cheese, goat cheese, or grilled sausage.

1 pint cherry tomatoes

3 garlic cloves
  or ¼ small onion

1 fresh medium hot chili
  pepper, such as serrano
  or Fresno

3 tablespoons extra-virgin
  olive oil

Fine sea salt

6 large eggs

Fresh cilantro, for garnish

Chili flakes, for garnish

Warm flatbread or toast,
  for serving

1   Cut the tomatoes into round slices. Thinly slice the garlic. If using, finely dice the onion. Thinly slice the chili pepper (remove the seeds for a milder flavor).

2   Heat a wide nonstick pan over medium heat. Once hot, pour the oil into the pan, then add the garlic or onion and the chili pepper and cook, stirring until fragrant and softened, about 1 minute for garlic or 2 to 3 minutes if using onion. Add the tomatoes, season with salt, and cook, stirring, until the tomatoes break down, 3 to 5 minutes.

3   Crack in the eggs around the pan. Cover and let everything cook in the sauce for about 5 minutes.

4   While the eggs cook, discard the stems and roughly chop the leaves of the cilantro. Once the yolks have reached the desired doneness, uncover and garnish with the cilantro and chili flakes.

5   Serve out of the pan with flatbread or toast on the side to scoop up the eggs.

roasted sukuma quiche

This quiche combines humble dishes inspired by one of my favorite lazy Kenyan dinners: sauteed collard greens (also called Sukuma Wiki, page 49) and ugali. Ugali is a white corn meal commonly eaten in several East African countries, quite similar to Italian polenta. Here the ugali is used to prepare a buttery short crust pastry filled with roasted vegetables that are typically used to prepare sukuma wiki.

For the Pastry Dough

1 cup all-purpose flour

⅓ cup white cornmeal

Fine sea salt

8 tablespoons (1 stick) unsalted butter, room temperature

3 tablespoons cold water

For the Roasted Vegetables

1 bundle collard greens

2 medium tomatoes

1 small red onion

Extra-virgin olive oil

Fine sea salt

For the Egg Filling

1 fresh medium hot chili pepper, such as serrano or Fresno

5 large eggs

1 cup half-and-half (or ½ cup milk and ½ cup cream)

Fine sea salt

1   Position a rack in the center of your oven, and preheat to 400°F (200°C).

2   **Make the pastry dough:** Cut the butter in small ½-inch pieces, keeping cold until ready to use. In a medium mixing bowl, combine the flour, cornmeal, and 1 teaspoon salt. Add the butter, and using your fingertips, incorporate everything until it's crumbly in texture. Slowly add the cold water to bring the dough together, then shape it into a ball. If you feel like your dough is too crumbly, carefully add another 1 tablespoon cold water. Wrap tightly in plastic wrap and chill in the fridge for 30 minutes. The dough will continue to hydrate while resting.

3   **Roast the vegetables:** Remove the hard stems from the collard greens. Layer them on top of one another and roll into a log, then roughly chop into 2-inch pieces. Cut the tomatoes and onion into wedges.

4   Arrange the collard greens, onion, and tomatoes on a baking sheet. Coat generously with oil and season with salt. Using your hands, mix the vegetables, ensuring everything is well coated in oil. Roast for 10 minutes, then flip the vegetables. Roast until the greens are crispy and the onion has softened, 5 to 10 minutes. Remove the veggies from the oven and lower the temperature to 350°F (180°C).

5   On a lightly floured work surface, roll out the
    chilled dough into a circle so the pastry will
    hang over the edges of a 9-inch pie dish. Place
    the dough into the pie dish and pinch or crimp
    the edges. Line the top with parchment paper
    and fill the crust with ceramic baking beans or
    other pie crust weights. Par-bake the crust for
    10 minutes in the center of the oven.

6   Once par-baked, remove the pie crust weight
    and arrange the greens at the bottom. Then
    add the tomatoes and onion on top.

7   **Make the egg filling:** Thinly slice the chili
    (remove the seeds for a milder flavor). In a
    large mixing bowl, whisk together the sliced
    chili, eggs, half-and-half, and a generous pinch
    of salt. Pour the egg mixture into the pie dish
    over the veggies.

8   Bake until the center is no longer wobbly, 25 to
    30 minutes. Cool for 15 minutes before slicing
    and serving.

africali rolex

A modern Ugandan street food, a rolex is an omelet rolled into a chapati (see pages 64 and 68). Typical toppings are kachumbari (a tomato salsa; see page 39) and shaved cabbage, but part of the fun is adding whatever you have on hand, which, for me, is typically leftovers. Whenever I make chapatis, I'm sure to put a couple to the side for a rolex the following day, but if I'm without chapatis, a flour tortilla does the job, too!

For Each Rolex

2 large eggs

Fine sea salt

1 tablespoon unsalted butter

1 chapati or large flour tortilla

Suggested Toppings (pick at least 2)

Spicy Tomato Jam (page 227)

Cherry Tomato Kachumbari (page 39)

Sliced avocado

Crispy bacon

Cooked sausage

Sautéed spinach with garlic and chili pepper flakes

Shaved cabbage

Sliced and salted tomato

Crumbled goat cheese or feta

1   Heat a 10-inch nonstick skillet over medium heat.

2   In a small bowl, whisk together the eggs and season with salt. Here you can add a small handful of vegetables or cheese, if using. When the pan is hot, melt the butter in the skillet, swirling around the pan to coat. The butter should be bubbly before you pour in the eggs. Gently shake the pan to keep the eggs from sticking.

3   Once the eggs are half set but still slightly gooey, place a chapati on top, gently pressing down so it sticks to the eggs. Cook for about 30 seconds before flipping with a spatula. Let the other side cook until the chapati is warmed through and the eggs are fully cooked, 30 seconds to 1 minute.

4   Use the spatula to slide the egg chapati onto a cutting board, egg side facing up. Scatter on any additional toppings.

5   Starting from the bottom edges closest to you, roll upward, finishing seam side facing down so it doesn't unravel. Cut in half to reveal the colorful cross section and enjoy!

chicken & okra wet fry

Most West African okra preparations lean into the slime, and there is even a dish in Nigeria nicknamed "draw soup" that describes the texture of the soup body. I have never been a fan of slimy okra, but luckily the Greeks have a trick for removing the excess moisture that the plant needs to grow in dry climates.

A wet fry is a common way of preparing meat in Kenya. Bite-size meat is sautéed with tomatoes and aromatics—and sometimes gently spiced—making it the perfect vehicle for a fresh okra dish. I like to serve my okra wet fry with rice, ugali (cooked white cornmeal), or polenta.

tip

Frozen defrosted okra can be used here. Reduce the cooking time as it won't be as firm as fresh okra.

½ pound fresh okra

½ cup white vinegar

1 tablespoon fine sea salt

Extra-virgin olive oil

1 pound boneless skinless chicken thighs

2 teaspoons Curry Powder (page 239)

1 medium onion

2 fresh medium hot chili peppers, such as serrano or Fresno

1 tablespoon Garlic Ginger Paste (page 231)

3 medium tomatoes

Small handful fresh cilantro, for garnish

1 In a small dish in which the ingredients will fit tightly, coat the okra in the vinegar and salt. Let it sit for at least 1 hour to draw out the moisture from the okra. Rinse well before using. Cut the okra in half lengthwise. The more cuts made to the okra, the more slime will be released.

2 Set a wide pan over medium-high heat, coating the bottom generously with oil. When the oil is shimmering, place the chicken in a single layer in the pan and let brown on all sides until crispy, 6 to 8 minutes. Season with salt and the curry powder, then cook to let them crisp up even more, 3 to 4 minutes. Remove the chicken and leave any extra oil behind in the pan. Set the chicken aside on a plate to rest.

3 Roughly chop the onion, add to the pan, and cook, stirring occasionally, until it starts to brown, about 3 minutes. Lower the heat to medium. Thinly slice the chili peppers (remove the seeds for a milder flavor) and slice the tomatoes into ½-inch wedges. Add the chilis and garlic ginger paste to the pan and cook, stirring until slightly brown, about 3 minutes.

4 Add the tomatoes and okra and cook, stirring occasionally, until the okra is bright green and slightly tender, about 5 minutes. Roughly chop the cilantro (leaves and stems). Thinly slice the chicken and add back into the pan, garnish with cilantro, and serve.

green curry with chicken & plantains

I learned how to make Thai green curry while filming the recipe with the chefs behind my favorite Thai restaurant in Los Angeles, Luv2Eat Thai. Adding blended fresh basil makes it much greener than what's typically served in restaurants. Semisweet plantain replaces pumpkin or squash, commonly found in vegetable-forward curries. Cooking the curry and plantains in separate pots keeps the curry liquid from becoming too thick from the plantain starch.

2 semi-ripe plantains

Fine sea salt

2 tightly packed cups fresh basil leaves, plus additional for garnish

5 tablespoons extra-virgin olive oil, divided

1 (14-ounce) can coconut milk, divided

½ medium red bell pepper

½ small eggplant

1 pound boneless skinless chicken thighs

¼ cup green curry paste

1 tablespoon sugar

1 tablespoon fish sauce

1 (4-ounce) can bamboo shoots

Cooked long-grain rice, for serving

1   Peel the plantains and cut them into 2-inch-long batons. Bring a large pot of salted water to a boil. Add the plantains and cook until tender, 5 to 7 minutes. Drain and set aside.

2   In a blender, add the basil with 3 tablespoons of oil and a splash of coconut milk, and blend until smooth. Set aside. Thinly slice the bell pepper. Trim the stem off the eggplant and cut it into 1-inch chunks. Cut the chicken into thin slices.

3   Heat a large saucepan over medium heat. Once hot, combine the remaining 2 tablespoons of oil and the curry paste and cook, stirring frequently until fragrant, about 1 minute.

4   Stir in the remaining coconut milk, the chicken, sugar, and fish sauce. Drain the can of bamboo shoots, then add the bamboo shoots, bell pepper, and eggplant to the pan, stir to combine, and cook until the pepper has slightly softened and the chicken has cooked through, about 15 minutes.

5   Stir in the basil oil, then turn off the heat and let it sit, covered, for 5 minutes to allow the flavors to infuse. Serve in bowls with rice and garnish with basil leaves.

kuku paka noodles

Curry and rice are a classic pairing. My take on the Swahili dish of grilled chicken (kuku) in coconut curry sauce is cut with broth and lime juice for a creamy, refreshing soup base that can be slurped up with the rice noodles. Cooking the noodles separately keeps them from becoming gummy during the cooking process and imparts no unwanted starch into the soup, keeping it at the right consistency.

1 pound boneless skinless chicken thighs

1 teaspoon fine sea salt

½ medium yellow onion

1 fresh medium hot chili pepper, such as serrano or Fresno

2 medium tomatoes

3 tablespoons coconut oil or extra-virgin olive oil, divided

1 tablespoon Garlic Ginger Paste (page 231)

2 tablespoons Curry Powder (page 239)

½ teaspoon ground turmeric

1 (14-ounce) can full-fat coconut milk, divided

1 cup chicken stock

Handful fresh cilantro

4 ounces dried rice noodles

Juice of 1 lime

1   Season the chicken thighs with the salt. Thinly slice the onion and chili pepper (remove the seeds for a milder flavor). Dice the tomatoes.

2   Heat 2 tablespoons of coconut oil in a wide braising pan or Dutch oven over medium-high heat. When the oil is shimmering, add the chicken in a single layer and cook until a deep golden brown, 3 to 4 minutes on each side. Set aside on a plate to rest.

3   Add the remaining 1 tablespoon of coconut oil to the same pot if it is dry, then add the onion and cook, stirring until translucent, 2 to 3 minutes. Lower the heat to medium, then stir in the chili pepper, tomatoes, garlic ginger paste, curry powder, turmeric, and a splash of the coconut milk.

4   Bring a separate pot of salted water to a boil.

5   Thinly slice the chicken and add to the curry along with the remaining coconut milk and chicken stock. Simmer for 15 minutes. Discard the stems of the cilantro and roughly chop the leaves, then place in a small bowl.

6   Cook the rice noodles in the pot of boiling salted water according to package directions. Drain the noodles and rinse well under cold water to prevent further cooking.

7   Divide the noodles among serving bowls. Take the curry off the heat. Squeeze in the lime juice and stir in the cilantro leaves, seasoning with salt to taste if needed.

8   Spoon the hot curry over the bowls of rice noodles and serve.

tips

Get that Swahili coast flavor by cooking the chicken on the grill before adding to the curry.

Keep the noodles and curry separate until you're ready to serve, otherwise the noodles will soak up all the curry sauce.

red pepper vodka chicken

Nigerian obe ata, aka stew, can be used as the foundation for building various dishes beyond Nigeria's borders. Here fresh tomatoes are swapped for tomato paste, and peppers are oven roasted, keeping the essence of the spicy tomato pepper sauce without having to reduce on the stovetop. This provides the base for a take on vodka sauce that pairs great with a short pasta.

6 to 8 boneless skinless chicken thighs

Fine sea salt

2 medium red bell peppers

3 shallots

4 garlic cloves

1 fresh very hot chili pepper, such as habanero or Scotch bonnet

3 tablespoons extra-virgin olive oil

3 tablespoons tomato paste

2 sprigs fresh oregano or 1 teaspoon dried oregano, plus 1 sprig fresh oregano, for garnish (optional)

¼ cup vodka

⅓ cup heavy cream

1 tablespoon unsalted butter

Cooked pasta or grains, for serving

1 Season the chicken thighs with salt and set aside.

2 Arrange a rack on the second highest shelf in the oven. Turn on the broiler to high.

3 Line a baking sheet with foil. Cut the bell peppers in half and discard the stem and seeds. Place face down on the prepared baking sheet and broil for about 10 minutes, or until the skin is blistered and blackened. Flip each pepper and broil until the edges start to char slightly, 5 to 7 minutes. Transfer the peppers

to a bowl and tightly cover with plastic wrap or foil to steam.

4 Turn off the broiler and carefully reposition the rack to the center. Preheat the oven to 400°F (200°C). Finely chop the shallots and thinly slice the garlic, then set aside in a bowl.

5 Once the bell peppers are cool enough to handle, peel and discard the papery charred skin. In a blender, add the bell peppers and chili pepper (remove the seeds for a milder flavor) and blend until smooth. Set aside in a bowl.

6 Heat the olive oil in a wide 12-inch oven-safe pan over medium-high heat. When the oil is shimmering, add the chicken in batches, if necessary, and cook until a deep golden brown, 3 to 5 minutes on each side; don't worry about cooking the chicken all the way through. Place the chicken on a plate to rest.

7 Lower the heat to medium. Add the shallots and garlic to the same pan and cook, stirring occasionally until the shallots have softened, about 5 minutes. Stir in the tomato paste and oregano and cook until the tomato paste darkens, 3 to 5 minutes.

8 Add the vodka to deglaze the pan, scraping the bottom with a wooden spoon to loosen any flavorful browned bits. Pour in the red pepper sauce and bring to a simmer. Stir in the cream and butter. Season with 1½ teaspoons salt, making sure to taste and adjust the salt as needed.

9 Arrange the chicken in the pan and transfer it to the oven for about 15 minutes, or until it has fully cooked.

10 Garnish with the oregano sprig, if using, and serve alongside your choice of pasta or grain.

yassa poulet summer rolls

My introduction to Senegalese food started with yassa. My college classmate Baye would whip up a pot of yassa poulet by simply cooking chicken, onions, oil, black pepper, lemon, and Dijon mustard together.

While traveling in Senegal, I found rice paper spring rolls sold in the markets. Fresh spring rolls are great for parties because they are served at room temperature. Though many parts of this recipe can be made from scratch, there is nothing wrong with a little semi-homemade help here and there, especially while entertaining.

2 medium yellow onions

3 garlic cloves

1 fresh very hot chili pepper, such as habanero or Scotch bonnet

2 tablespoons extra-virgin olive oil

½ rotisserie chicken or 1 pound cooked chicken meat

Juice of 2 lemons

2 tablespoons smooth Dijon mustard

¼ teaspoon freshly ground black pepper

Mango Sweet Chili Sauce (page 226), for serving

1 package rice spring roll wrappers

Suggested Toppings
4 green onions, sliced

½ head green cabbage, finely shredded

1 bundle fresh mint leaves, roughly chopped (remove stems)

½ bundle fresh cilantro, roughly chopped (leaves and stems)

2 medium bell peppers (yellow, red, or orange), thinly sliced

2 cucumbers, cut into thin matchsticks

1 Finely chop the onions, garlic, and chili pepper (remove the seeds for a milder flavor). Heat a saucepan over medium heat. Once hot (sprinkle a few drops of water into the pan—the water should sizzle and evaporate quickly), pour the oil into the saucepan, add the chopped onions, garlic, and chili pepper and cook, stirring occasionally, until the onions begin to soften, about 5 minutes.

2 Shred the chicken, discarding any skin and bones (if using rotisserie—you can save these in the freezer to use for stock). Add the chicken to the pan. Stir in the lemon juice,

mustard, and black pepper. Cover with a lid and let cook until the veggies have fully softened, about 5 minutes.

3 Arrange all the toppings on a platter so guests can make their own. Serve the chicken with the mango sweet chili sauce for dipping and the rice spring roll wrappers.

How To Wrap:

4 To soften the spring roll wrappers, dip them one at a time into a plate covered with a layer of lukewarm water.

5   Assemble the spring roll by adding a bit of the chicken and each of your extra toppings to the center of the wrapper. Don't be tempted to overfill, otherwise the wrapper will tear. Roll the same way you would a burrito: fold in the left and right sides toward the center, then bring the bottom of the wrapper over the filling and wrap tightly by rolling it upward.

roast chicken with poussin sauce

Fast food chicken may be the best, or perhaps a close second to burgers. Nairobi's take involves chicken and chips (fries), where roasted chickens are chopped up and flash fried to order, then served with what seems to be never enough poussin sauce. The sauce in question is made of spiced butter with lemon juice, and it's spicy, refreshing, and indulgent all at the same time. Setting up a pot of oil for a thirty-second fry isn't practical for home cooking, so a well-roasted chicken is more than enough.

For the Roast Chicken

1 (4-pound) whole chicken

Fine sea salt

4 garlic cloves

2 teaspoons dried oregano, divided

3 tablespoons unsalted butter or extra-virgin olive oil

For the Poussin Sauce

4 tablespoons (½ stick) unsalted butter

1 tablespoon Garlic Ginger Paste (page 231)

2 teaspoons ground smoked paprika

1½ teaspoons chili powder (Kashmiri preferred)

1 teaspoon fine sea salt

½ teaspoon sugar

Juice of 1 lemon

1   **Make the roast chicken:** Position a rack in the upper-middle of your oven, and preheat to 425°F (220°C).

2   Place the chicken on a flat surface with the back side up. Using your fingers, find where the spine is, and using sharp kitchen scissors, cut out the spine, then discard. Flip the chicken over to breast side up, and using the palm of your hand, firmly press down on the chicken and flatten.

3   Season the chicken with 1 teaspoon salt on each side and let it sit skin side up at room temperature for at least 1 hour.

4   Thinly slice the garlic and mix in a small bowl with ¼ teaspoon salt, ¼ teaspoon of oregano, and the butter.

5   Pat the chicken dry with a paper towel. Loosen the chicken skin with your fingers and and stuff the skin with the garlic herb mix, rubbing any extra on the outside. Roast in the oven for 45 minutes, or until the internal temperature of thickest part of the chicken breast reaches 160°F (70°C).

6   **Make the poussin sauce:** Melt the butter in a small saucepan set over medium heat. Add the garlic ginger paste and cook, stirring occasionally, until it has fully incorporated into the sauce, 2 to 3 minutes. Stir in the

paprika, chili powder, salt, and sugar just until all the spices have dissolved into the sauce, about 1 minute. Turn off the heat and stir in the lemon juice.

7   When you're ready to serve, brush the top of the chicken with the poussin sauce and serve with any extra poussin sauce on the side.

tips

If your grocery store has a butcher counter, ask them to spatchcock the chicken for you.

If you spatchcock the chicken yourself, keep the spine in the freezer to use for chicken stock!

If you're hosting, precarve the chicken once it is finished and arrange on a serving platter, before pouring the poussin sauce over the slices and serving.

coriander katsu chicken

Chicken, pounded, tossed in breadcrumbs, and fried, is always a good move. Known in Japan as katsu chicken, it's quick to prepare and gives the satisfaction of fried chicken, but with a fast cook time. The aroma in the seeded crust awakens as it's fried, providing tiny pops of flavor with each bite.

Kachumbari, a tomato salad, is typically served alongside meat dishes in East Africa, with the acidity contrasting the saltiness and fattiness of the protein. Though any tomato can be used, I like the sweetness cherry tomatoes add.

tip
Katsu chicken makes for a killer fried chicken sandwich!

---

4 boneless skinless chicken thighs

Fine sea salt

½ cup all-purpose flour

Handful fresh cilantro

2 large eggs

1½ cups panko breadcrumbs

1 tablespoon cumin seeds

1 tablespoon coriander seeds

Neutral oil, such as avocado oil or extra-light olive oil, for frying

Cherry Tomato Kachumbari (page 39)

---

1   Pound out the chicken thighs until they are ¼-inch thick, place on a plate, and season with salt.

2   Set out three shallow bowls. In the first bowl, place the flour. Discard the stems from the cilantro and roughly chop the leaves. In the second bowl, whisk together the eggs and cilantro. In the third bowl, combine the panko, cumin seeds, and coriander seeds.

3   Dip the chicken in the bowl of flour, making sure the chicken is coated all over. Doing this will give the egg a better surface to cling to, so your coating sticks better!

4   Working one piece at a time, shake off the excess flour, dip into the egg bowl, and then into the breadcrumbs bowl, coating well for each step. Repeat with the remaining pieces.

5   Allow the chicken to rest on a plate for 10 minutes so the breadcrumbs have time to stick to the chicken before frying.

6   Heat about ½ inch neutral oil in a large pan to 350°F (180°C). Line a plate with paper towels and place it beside the stove. When the oil is ready, fry the chicken pieces in batches to not overcrowd the pan. Fry on one side, 2 to 3 minutes, flip the chicken pieces and cook the other side until browned, 2 to 3 minutes. Place the chicken pieces on the paper towel–lined plate to drain the excess oil, then transfer the chicken to a wire rack so it doesn't become soggy.

7   Serve with a generous scoop of kachumbari on top.

peri-peri garlic butter shrimp

Any food cooked on an open flame has big potential to be delicious. Shrimp are simple—just do not overcook them! Butterflied shrimp are great for two reasons: they're an easy way to devein the shrimp and it gives you maximum surface area for any seasoning. The star here is the garlicky spicy peri-peri butter that gets basted on top of the salty charred shrimp. Well, I guess the only other misstep here is not having some bread to mop up all the delicious butter off the plate.

tip
This makes a great share plate or appetizer served alongside some warm grilled bread.

1 pound jumbo shell-on shrimp, about 18 (with or without heads)

Fine sea salt

1 to 2 tablespoons extra-virgin olive oil

4 tablespoons Peri-Peri Butter (page 232), plus more for serving

Juice of 2 limes

Lime wedges, for serving

1 Carefully cut halfway through the back of the shrimp to butterfly, keeping the head intact (if using whole shrimp). Remove the dark vein and discard. Repeat with all the shrimp, then lightly salt and coat in 1 tablespoon of oil.

Grill Method

2 Melt the peri-peri butter and set aside. Heat the grill to medium-high heat. Make sure there are no active flames when it's ready to use. Once hot, place the shrimp on the grill; there should be a ½ inch space between each shrimp so it is easy to turn them over.

3 Sear until slightly charred on all sides and the shrimp have turned bright pink, 2 to 4 minutes each side. The cook time will depend on how direct the heat is under the shrimp.

4 Using a silicone pastry brush, lightly brush the shrimp with the peri-peri butter before removing from the grill. Transfer to a serving platter, squeeze over the lime juice, and brush with more melted peri-peri butter. Serve warm with lime wedges and extra melted peri-peri butter on the side for dipping.

Stovetop Method

2 Heat a cast-iron pan on the stove over medium-high heat. Once the pan starts to smoke, lower to a medium heat and pour 1 tablespoon olive oil into the pan, then add the shrimp; there should be a ½ inch space between each shrimp to not overcrowd the pan. Sear until slightly charred on all sides and the shrimp have turned bright pink, 2 to 3 minutes each side.

3 Lower the heat to low and add in the peri-peri butter. Toss to well coat the shrimp in the butter. Once the butter is fully melted, turn off the heat and add the lime juice. Serve warm with lime wedges and extra melted peri-peri butter on the side for dipping.

yassa poisson

Serves 4

I don't think a day went by in Senegal where I didn't eat some kind of yassa dish. My best plate of yassa was after a walking tour of Gorée, a small island off the coast of Dakar. We sat down for lunch and ordered shrimp, yassa poulet (chicken), and yassa poisson (fish). The fish was cooked on the grill, then topped with heaps of Dijon-laced lemony yassa onions. I haven't forgotten it since.

4 boneless and skinless salmon fillets

Fine sea salt

2 medium onions

1 fresh very hot chili pepper, such as habanero or Scotch bonnet

⅓ cup pitted green olives

2 tablespoons Dijon mustard

½ teaspoon sweet paprika

1 lemon, halved

Extra-virgin olive oil

½ cup of vegetable stock, chicken stock, or water

Cooked rice or couscous, for serving

1 Pat the salmon dry using a paper towel, then season with salt on both sides and set aside.

2 Thinly slice the onions. Finely dice the chili pepper (remove the seeds for a milder flavor) and green olives. Place the onions, chili pepper, green olives, mustard, and paprika into a bowl. Add in the juice of one half of the lemon and mix to combine.

3 Generously coat the bottom of a wide frying pan with oil and set over medium-high heat. When the oil is shimmering, add the onion mixture and cook until the mixture has lightly browned, 8 to 10 minutes. Stir in the vegetable stock, bring to a simmer, and cook until the onions have softened, 3 to 5 minutes; cover with a lid if the sauce is thickening too quickly. Season with salt to taste. Transfer to a bowl and set aside.

4 Using the same pan, lower the heat to medium heat and generously coat the bottom with oil. When the oil is shimmering, add the salmon fillets. Avoid touching the fish while it cooks so it can develop the best crust; after a crust has formed on one side of the fillets, about 5 minutes, flip and cook until both sides are golden and the flesh of the fish has lightened in color, 3 to 5 minutes. Squeeze the juice of the remaining lemon half over the fish.

5 Spoon the yassa onions on top of the salmon fillets and serve with rice or couscous.

121

AfriCali

beef, lamb & pork

harissa chili

They say a good chili needs time. Well, that is true for all stews, but a properly spiced chili with mouth-watering toppings can still get a delicious meal on the table without having to stir a pot all day.

tip
Switch things up and try this with ground lamb!

1 medium onion

1-inch piece fresh ginger

6 garlic cloves

2 fresh medium hot chili peppers, such as serrano or Fresno

3 tablespoons extra-virgin olive oil

1 pound ground beef

2 teaspoons ground cumin

1 teaspoon ground coriander seeds

1 teaspoon smoked paprika

2 teaspoons fine sea salt, plus more as needed

1½ cups beef stock

1 (14-ounce) can diced tomatoes

2 tablespoons rose harissa (see page 222), plus more for serving

Handful fresh cilantro

1 (14-ounce) can black-eyed peas

1 cup sour cream or plain thick yogurt

1   Finely dice the onion. Peel and grate the ginger. Thinly slice the garlic. Thinly slice the chili peppers (remove the seeds for a milder flavor) and set half aside for garnish.

2   Heat the oil in a medium pot over medium-high heat. When the oil is shimmering, add the beef. Using a wooden spoon, break the beef into small pieces. Once the beef begins to crisp up, 3 to 5 minutes, add the onion and cook, stirring occasionally until translucent, 2 to 3 minutes. Add the ginger, garlic, chili peppers, cumin, coriander seeds, paprika, and salt and cook, stirring frequently, until fragrant, about 1 minute. Stir in the stock, the tomatoes and

their liquid, and the harissa. Bring the mixture to a boil, then reduce the heat to a simmer.

3   Roughly chop the cilantro. Stir the stems into the chili, and place leaves into a small bowl.

4   Drain and rinse the black-eyed peas, then stir them into the beef mixture and cook, partially covered, for at least 45 minutes, stirring occasionally to prevent burning on the bottom. Season with salt to taste before serving.

5   Serve in individual bowls and top with the sour cream, harissa, the reserved chili peppers, and the cilantro.

berbere braised short ribs

Ethiopian berbere is easily the most used spice blend in my kitchen. As an essential in the nation's most popular dishes, each cook has their own combination that always has dried peppers as the foundation. Berbere can be found online, in any Ethiopian grocery store, or in the spice aisle of shops like World Market, Whole Foods, and gourmet markets. It works wonders in slow-cooked dishes like these braised short ribs, which are cooked fork-tender, but never too soft like pulled beef. "Mush meat" has always been a big NO-NO in my family. For Maasai people, meat is essential and must be treated preciously. To cook meat into oblivion is an act of treason. This dish is best served in bowls, alongside mashed potatoes or any grain.

tip
If you have any leftovers, enjoy the next day for lunch in lettuce wraps or tacos.

2 pounds boneless short ribs or chuck

Fine sea salt

Coarsely ground black pepper

4 garlic cloves

1-inch piece fresh ginger

2 medium red onions

3 tablespoons neutral oil, such as avocado or peanut oil

3 tablespoons Spiced Ghee (page 235) or plain ghee or unsalted butter

1½ tablespoons berbere spice

2 tablespoons tomato paste

2 cups beef stock

¼ cup pomegranate seeds, for garnish

1 Cut the short ribs into big 3-inch chunks. Season generously with salt and black pepper on all sides. Set aside and let rest, at room temperature, for at least 1 hour.

2 Position a rack in the center of your oven, and preheat to 325°F (160°C).

3 Peel the garlic cloves and ginger. Blitz the garlic and ginger in a small food processor or blender until finely chopped. Scrape into a bowl and set aside. Add the onions to the food processor and pulse to a small dice. Set aside.

4 Heat the oil in an oven-safe braising pot or Dutch oven over medium-high heat. When the oil is shimmering, working in batches, sear the beef on all sides to develop a golden-brown crust. Set the seared beef on a plate to rest.

5 Lower the heat to medium. Add the diced onions to the same pan with the rendered beef fat and cook, stirring occasionally to prevent burning, until soft and dark brown, 15 to 20 minutes.

6 Add the spiced ghee, berbere spice, tomato paste, and the minced garlic and ginger. Cook, stirring frequently, until the garlic is fragrant, about 2 minutes.

7 Stir in the beef stock. Bring the sauce to a simmer and return the beef to the pan. Reduce the heat to medium-low and cover with a lid.

8 Roast in the oven until the beef easily breaks apart with two forks, 1½ to 2 hours. Divide the braised beef among your serving plates and garnish with the pomegranate seeds.

berburger pasta

As a young cook, meal starter kits made me feel like I could prepare a real meal without asking for an adult's help with a knife. Hamburger Helper felt a step above boxed mac and cheese because I got to brown the beef before seasoning it with the mystery spice packet. Though I haven't touched a box since I got full rein over the kitchen, the concept of a cheeseburger-inspired pasta still sounds delicious! I first made this using leftover Ethiopian takeout, and the fusion instantly brought together two very nostalgic flavors.

tip

Store leftovers in the fridge in an airtight container. Reheat on the stove with a splash of milk to make the sauce creamy again.

Fine sea salt

1 medium onion

Extra-virgin olive oil

1 tablespoon Garlic Ginger Paste (page 231)

1 teaspoon cumin seeds

2 tablespoons berbere spice

1 pound 85/15 ground beef

½ pound short pasta, such as fusilli

3 tablespoons tomato paste

½ cup dry red wine

1 tablespoon chickpea flour (optional)

1 cup whole milk

2 cups shredded sharp Cheddar cheese

½ cup grated Parmesan cheese

1   Fill a large pot halfway with water and salt generously. Set over high heat to bring to a boil.

2   Chop the onion into a fine dice. Set a braising pan over medium heat. Once hot, put a splash of olive oil into the pan, then add the onion and cook, stirring occasionally with a wooden spoon until soft, 3 to 5 minutes. Add the garlic ginger paste, cumin seeds, and berbere spice and cook, stirring frequently until fragrant, about 2 minutes.

3   Add the beef and break it into small pieces using the wooden spoon. Increase the heat to medium-high and continue to cook the beef, stirring occasionally, until browned.

4   While the beef is cooking, cook the pasta in the salted boiling water. Set a timer according to the package directions and reserve 1 cup of pasta water before draining.

5   Once the beef has browned, stir in the tomato paste and cook until it turns a darker red, 1 to 2 minutes. Lower the heat to medium, pour in the wine, and use the wooden spoon to scrape up any browned bits from the bottom of the pan.

6   Sprinkle in the chickpea flour, if using, and stir well to ensure there are no clumps. Stir in the milk and the Cheddar and Parmesan cheeses. Once the cheeses have partially melted, fold in the cooked pasta. If the sauce is too thick, add small splashes of the reserved pasta water.

mom's steak with capers

My mom picked up this recipe when she was at a friend's house in Marin County, California. Once she made it for me, I kept asking for it "again"—my favorite word as a child. Typically served with fluffy basmati rice and sautéed veggies (like the Broccolini with Gingery Peas, page 43), this recipe is incredibly simple to prepare, and still, to this day, I let this be my mom's dish for her to make.

1 pound skirt steak	**2 tablespoons vegetable oil**	**1½ tablespoons capers**
Fine sea salt	**⅓ cup beef stock**	**1 teaspoon unsalted butter**
Freshly ground black pepper	**2 tablespoons Dijon mustard**	

1 Season the steak with salt and black pepper. Heat the oil in a frying pan over medium-high heat. When the oil is shimmering, add the steak and sear until a crust forms, 4 to 5 minutes on each side; the cook time will depend on the thickness of the steak, so check the underside a few times during cooking.

2 Remove the steak, leaving the juices in the pan, and allow it to rest for 10 minutes before slicing.

3 While the steak rests, lower the heat to medium. To the frying pan, add the stock, mustard, capers, and butter and simmer until the sauce is thick and heated through, 2 to 3 minutes.

4 Spoon the sauce over the sliced steak before serving.

mishkaki party

Mishkaki is a style of kebab—or small cubes of skewered marinated meat—served on the Swahili coast. My first time eating mishkaki was in the northern part of Mombasa, in a local eatery where the meat hits your table within seconds of it being pulled off the charcoal grill. The accompaniments are simple because the meat is the star. Any meat can be used here; just be sure to use tender cuts, as they will cook quickly on the grill.

tip
Use shorter skewers if cooking your mishkaki indoors so they can easily fit in your pan.

2 pounds of tender meat (New York steak, boneless skinless chicken thighs, or tender lamb)

2 teaspoons fine sea salt

2 tablespoons Garlic Ginger Paste (page 231)

2 tablespoons neutral oil, such as avocado or peanut oil

2 teaspoons ground turmeric

1 to 2 teaspoons chili powder (Kashmiri preferred)

2 teaspoons ground cumin or coriander

Juice of 2 limes

2 dozen skewers

1 Cut the meat into ½-inch cubes; it's easier to cut if the meat is chilled first. Combine the salt, garlic ginger paste, oil, turmeric, chili powder, cumin, and lime juice in a large bowl and mix well. Toss in the meat into the mix to coat well and let it sit for at least 1 hour to overnight.

2 If using wooden skewers, soak them in water for 1 hour before using. On each skewer, place 4 to 5 pieces of the meat, keeping them near the tip so the base can be used to turn them.

3 Heat a grill (or a cast-iron skillet if cooking indoors). Once hot, use a small amount of oil to grease the cooking surface lightly, then cook the skewers on the grill or skillet until lightly charred on all sides and cooked through; the cook time will vary depending on the type of meat and level of preferred doneness.

pili pili beef fry with green beans

Stir-fries are one of the most fun dishes to make. Sure, you will need the exhaust fan on, and you should probably crack open some windows, but there is something about tossing a pan of sizzling food that makes you feel like you're really cooking. The "pili pili" comes from the fresh chilis, so adjust to taste accordingly.

1 pound beef sirloin

Fine sea salt

½ pound trimmed green beans

6 garlic cloves

4 green onions

2 fresh medium hot chili peppers, such as serrano or Fresno

1-inch piece fresh ginger

Extra-virgin olive oil

1½ teaspoons Butcher's Masala (page 238) or garam masala

3 tablespoons Spiced Ghee (page 235)

Freshly ground black pepper

2 tablespoons soy sauce

Juice of 1 lime

Cooked rice or grains, for serving

1   Cut the beef into very thin slices (see Tip). Lightly season with salt and set aside. Cut the green beans into 2-inch-long pieces. Thinly slice the garlic, green onions, chili peppers (remove the seeds for a milder flavor), and ginger. Reserve a handful of the green onions and chilis for garnish.

2   Generously coat the bottom of a wide frying pan with oil and set over medium-high heat. When the oil is shimmering, add the beef. Cook, stirring occasionally, until the beef has browned, 5 to 7 minutes. Add the green beans and cook, stirring occasionally, until slightly softened, 3 to 5 minutes.

3   Lower the heat to medium and add the masala, garlic, green onions, chili peppers, and ginger. Season with salt and black pepper to

taste and cook, stirring, until the garlic has softened and is fragrant, 2 to 3 minutes. Stir in the soy sauce. Turn off the heat and stir in the lime juice.

4   Serve in individual bowls over rice or your choice of grain, and garnish with the reserved green onions and chilis.

tips

Chilled meat is easier to slice thin, so pop the steak in the freezer for an hour before cooking.

This is also delicious with egg noodles— just add your cooked noodles to the pan along with the aromatics and spices for a one-pan meal.

short ribs in stew

If Nigeria had a mother sauce, Obe Ata, aka pepper stew, would be it. It serves as the base for so many Nigerian staples such as Jollof Rice (page 76) but is also a meal on its own. The crucial step in creating a deeply flavored and rich stew is "frying" the sauce; a concept that initially confused my high school self. Here, to help the sauce reach its full potential, fatty short ribs replace what would otherwise be heaps of oil.

tip
Don't be tempted to drain the rendered fat from the beef! This helps the stew reduce and deepen in flavor.

For the Beef
4 pounds bone-in beef short ribs, at room temperature (3 pounds boneless)

Fine sea salt

Freshly ground black pepper

2 tablespoons neutral oil, such as avocado or peanut oil

1 medium onion

2 tablespoons Garlic Ginger Paste (page 231)

2 teaspoons Curry Powder (page 239)

1 teaspoon dried thyme

For the Stew Base
2 medium onions

1 medium red bell pepper

1 fresh very hot chili pepper, such as habanero or Scotch bonnet

1 cup beef stock

1 (14-ounce) can diced tomatoes or 6 fresh Roma tomatoes

1 **Prepare the beef:** Season the beef generously on all sides with salt and black pepper. Keep the short ribs at room temperature for 30 minutes before cooking.

2 Position a rack in the center of your oven, and preheat to 325°F (160°C).

3 **Make the stew base:** Roughly chop the onions, bell pepper, and chili pepper (remove the seeds for a milder flavor), and tomatoes if using fresh ones. Add to a blender with the beef stock and the diced tomatoes with their liquid, then blend until smooth. Set aside.

4 **Make the beef:** Heat the oil in an oven-safe braising dish or Dutch oven over medium-high heat. When the oil is shimmering, working in batches, add the short ribs and cook on all sides until they each have a golden crust; they will finish cooking in the stew later. Set aside on a plate. (See Tips.)

5 Slice the onion. Add the onion to the braising pan and cook in the rendered beef fat, stirring occasionally, until softened and browned on the edges, 5 to 8 minutes. Add the garlic ginger paste, curry powder, and dried thyme and cook, stirring frequently, until fragrant, 1 to 2 minutes.

6 Pour in the stew base mixture and simmer, scraping the bottom of the pan to incorporate any browned bits, 5 to 7 minutes. Add the short ribs bone-side facing up.

7 Cover with a lid or foil and cook in the oven, 2 to 2½ hours, or until the meat has reached desired tenderness. For the final 30 minutes of cooking, turn the beef, so the bone side is now facing down and cook uncovered so the tops can brown. Serve straight from the pot, roughly breaking up the beef chunks with a fork before serving.

lamb meatballs with tomatoes & chickpeas

Meatballs are greatly underappreciated. Minced meat gives you the maximum surface area for seasoning, and when cooked right, meatballs are tender, juicy meat parcels. Simmered in an aromatic tomato sauce, these meatballs can be scooped up with fluffy flatbread or enjoyed with couscous, rice, or even pasta.

1 medium onion

1 teaspoon cumin seeds

1 (14-ounce) can chickpeas

3 tablespoons extra-virgin olive oil, plus additional for mixing and shaping

1 pound ground lamb

¾ cup plain breadcrumbs

½ cup whole milk

2 large eggs

1 tablespoon garam masala

Fine sea salt

Handful fresh cilantro

1 tablespoon Garlic Ginger Paste (page 231)

1 (14-ounce) can diced tomatoes

1   Thinly slice the onion. With a mortar and pestle or a rolling pin, crush the cumin seeds to release more of their flavor. Drain and rinse the chickpeas.

2   Heat a wide frying pan over medium heat. Once hot, put the oil into the frying pan. Add the onion and cumin seeds and cook, stirring occasionally, until the onion has softened, 8 to 10 minutes.

3   While the onion is cooking, prepare the meatball filling. In a large mixing bowl, place the lamb, breadcrumbs, milk, eggs, garam masala, and 1 teaspoon salt. Roughly chop the cilantro (leaves and stems) and add to the bowl.

4   Once the onion has softened, stir in the garlic ginger paste and cook, stirring frequently, until fragrant, 1 to 2 minutes. Turn off the heat and divide the mixture, adding half to the

meatball filling and the rest to a small bowl. Set aside the frying pan to use later.

5   Line a large plate with plastic wrap. Lightly oil your hands and mix the meatball mixture until well combined. If needed, oil your hands again and shape the mixture into 18 meatballs, placing each ball on the prepared plate.

6   Heat the frying pan on medium-high and splash in some oil. Add the meatballs, brown them on all sides, and cook through, about 10 minutes. Remove the meatballs from the pan and set aside on a plate.

7   Lower the heat to medium and add the remaining browned aromatics. Add the diced tomatoes with their liquid, and the drained chickpeas, and season to taste with salt. Bring to a simmer. Add back in the meatballs and simmer over low heat for 10 minutes until ready to serve.

rosemary suya lamb chops

Delicate lamb chops are encrusted with aromatic yaji—suya spice— for one of my favorite special occasion meals. Feel free to scale up this recipe, because no matter how few people we are, it never seems to be enough. Made from peanuts with spices and ginger, yaji isn't one of those spices you lightly sprinkle onto your food. When preparing suya, the popular Nigerian grilled meat skewers, the meat gets three hits of spice: once before grilling, second after they come off the grill, and a side for you to dip into.

2 lamb racks (1½ pounds each)

Fine sea salt

6 garlic cloves

3 fresh rosemary sprigs

6 tablespoons Yaji (page 242), divided

¼ cup extra-virgin olive oil, divided

½ teaspoon sea salt flakes

1 Cut the lamb into individual chops. Generously salt the chops with fine sea salt and let them sit for 1 hour at room temperature.

2 In a blender or by hand, mince the garlic, rosemary leaves, 5 tablespoons of yaji, and 3 tablespoons of olive oil until a paste forms. Generously coat the lamb with the paste.

3 In a separate bowl, combine the remaining 1 tablespoon of yaji with the sea salt flakes.

4 Heat a cast-iron skillet or a grill over medium-high heat. Use the remaining olive oil to grease the cooking surface lightly. Cook the chops until golden brown, 2 to 3 minutes on each side. Serve warm with the salted yaji on the side for dipping.

berbere brown sugar bacon

This recipe came about after filming a video for the Berbere Braised Pork Tacos (page 154) at my studio when a crew member had the clever idea of putting the brown sugar mix on bacon. It quickly became a studio favorite and my new standard for cooking bacon.

1½ tablespoons brown sugar

2 teaspoons berbere spice

½ teaspoon freshly ground black pepper

1 pound bacon

1   Preheat the oven to 450°F (230°C).

2   In a small bowl, combine the brown sugar, berbere spice, and black pepper.

3   Double layer foil on a baking sheet. Arrange the bacon on the foil, making sure none of the slices overlap. Sprinkle on the spice rub from high up to distribute it evenly over the bacon.

4   Place the bacon in the oven on the lower or middle rack and cook for 10 to 15 minutes, depending on the desired doneness; 12 minutes is perfect in my oven to have some dark edges and not be flimsy.

5   Line a plate with paper towels and when the bacon is finished, transfer the slices to the plate to drain excess grease before serving.

berbere braised pork tacos

I have only had one real go at working in restaurants, and it was at a pop-up restaurant I held while studying for my publishing master's in London. From constantly studying food media, I wanted to create a tangible experience. So, like any American abroad, I did what reminded me of home. Having grown up in Oakland, California, there were two things I ate a lot of: Ethiopian food and tacos.

For the Spiced Pulled Pork

2 pounds boneless pork shoulder

Fine sea salt

Freshly ground black pepper

1 large yellow onion

6 garlic cloves

2 tablespoons neutral oil, such as avocado or peanut oil

3 tablespoons berbere spice

2 teaspoons whole cumin seeds

1½ teaspoons dried oregano

2 bay leaves

Juice of 1 large orange

6 ounces lager beer

2 tablespoons brown sugar

For the Tacos

2 ripe avocados

½ cup queso fresco or feta cheese

Pickled Red Onions (page 227)

Handful fresh cilantro

12 warm tortillas, such as corn, flour, or crispy taco shells

1 Position a rack in the center of your oven, and preheat to 325°F (160°C).

2 **Make the spiced pulled pork:** Cut the pork into large chunks, around 3 inches each. Season all sides of the pork generously with salt and black pepper. Let sit at room temperature for at least 30 minutes. Thinly slice the onion and garlic.

3 Heat the oil in an oven-safe braising dish or Dutch oven over medium-high heat. When the oil is shimmering, working in batches, sear the pork to a deep golden brown on all sides; they do not need to be fully cooked. Set the browned pork pieces on a plate to rest.

4 Lower the heat to medium. Add the onion and garlic to the same pan and cook, stirring occasionally, until the onion has softened, 5 to 7 minutes. Stir in the berbere spice, cumin seeds, oregano, and bay leaves. Add the orange

juice and the beer. Using a wooden spoon, scrape up any browned bits from the bottom of the pan.

5 Add the pork back to the pan in a single layer, cover, and cook in the oven until it easily pulls apart, 2½ to 3 hours.

6 **Make the tacos:** Prepare a platter with the taco ingredients shortly before serving. Thinly slice the avocados, crumble the cheese, drain the pickled onions from the brine, and remove the stems before roughly chopping the cilantro leaves.

7 Remove the pork from the oven and sprinkle with the brown sugar. Using two forks, lightly shred the pork, being sure to leave bite-size pieces of meat. Toss the pork in the braising liquid to coat well and serve with the taco platter and warm tortillas for build-your-own tacos.

spicy sausage, couscous, lentil & kale soup

We all have a dish that ages alongside us. As time goes on, certain ingredients get changed or upgraded, and the recipe is naturally fine-tuned. For me, dried tortellini became couscous, and white beans swapped for lentils, but the kale and sausage always stayed. The most significant change was the addition of the herby and spicy harissa floating on top, which gets into every bite of soup as the spoon passes through it.

1 pound raw spicy Italian sausage

1 cup cherry or grape tomatoes

2 tablespoons extra-virgin olive oil

½ cup dry white wine

2 quarts chicken stock

1 to 2 chicken bouillon cubes (optional)

¾ cup pearl couscous

1 (14-ounce) can cooked black or brown lentils

1½ cups Tuscan kale

¼ cup Herby Harissa (page 228)

1 Remove the sausage from its casing and discard the casing. Cut the cherry tomatoes into quarters.

2 Heat a Dutch oven or large pot over medium-high heat. Once hot, put the oil into the pan, then add the sausage. Using a wooden spoon, break the sausage into small pieces. Once the sausage begins to brown, 3 to 5 minutes, add the cherry tomatoes and cook, stirring occasionally, until the tomatoes begin to break down, 3 to 5 minutes.

3 Pour in the white wine, scraping up any brown bits from the bottom of the pot, and cook until completely reduced, 1 to 2 minutes. Transfer the mixture to a bowl and set aside.

4 Add the stock to the same pot, cover, and bring to a boil. Before adding the couscous, taste the stock. If it's too bland, add up to 2 chicken bouillon cubes (2 tablespoons powder), if using, or season with salt to taste. Add the couscous and partially cover to cook, leaving a small opening so it doesn't boil over. Set a timer and cook for 2 minutes less than the recommended time on the package.

5 While the couscous cooks, drain and rinse the can of cooked lentils. Remove any thick stalks from the kale. Finely chop the kale into small pieces that fit easily on a spoon. Once the timer goes off, add the kale, the browned sausage and tomato mixture, and the lentils and simmer for 5 minutes before removing from the heat.

6 Serve in bowls with a generous spoonful of herby harissa on top, placing the remaining herby harissa on the table for self-service.

sweets

&

drinks

coconut & cardamom mandazi

There are two names for fried dough in Kenya: mahamri and mandazi. The differences come down to the spices, but naming is more or less regional. Mandazi is the name I grew up with, but the use of cardamom here is typical of a coastal mahamri. Regardless of location, Kenyans enjoy this spiced fried dough with a hot cuppa Chai (page 205). Mandazi is similar to the New Orleans–style beignets but with more spice. A dusting of powdered sugar on top isn't typical of the East African donut, but the folks in New Orleans got it right when it comes to the finishing touch.

2½ teaspoons (1 envelope) active dry yeast

2 tablespoons plus ½ teaspoon granulated sugar, divided

¼ cup warm water

4 cups (520 grams) all-purpose flour, plus more as needed

2 teaspoons ground cardamom

½ teaspoon fine sea salt

2 tablespoons unsalted butter

1 (14-ounce) can coconut milk

Neutral oil, such as avocado or peanut oil, for frying

Powdered sugar, for garnish

1   In a large bowl, dissolve the yeast and ¼ teaspoon of sugar in the warm water; make sure that the water is not too hot or it will kill the yeast. Set aside for 10 minutes to allow the yeast to bloom.

2   Combine the flour, cardamom, salt, and the remaining sugar in a medium bowl.

3   Microwave the butter in a heatproof dish in 15-second increments until fully melted or melt in a small pan over high heat. Set aside to cool for a few minutes, then add to the bowl of yeast along with the coconut milk.

4   Using a wooden spoon, slowly incorporate the flour mixture into the liquid until thoroughly combined. The dough will be very sticky. Cover with a clean and slightly damp tea towel and leave in a warm place for 1 hour to rise.

5   Once the dough has doubled in volume, turn it out onto a clean and lightly floured worktop and shape into a ball; use plenty of flour to stop it from sticking to your hands or the worktop. Roll out the dough into a ¼-inch-thick rectangle and cut into 24 pieces.

6   Fill a pot with 1 inch oil and set over medium-high heat until it reaches 350°F (180°C). Line a baking tray with paper towels and place it beside the stove.

7   Working in batches to not overcrowd the pan, fry the mandazi until they puff up and are golden brown. As you fry, keep an eye on the oil temperature and adjust as needed to maintain the same temperature. Using a spider or slotted spoon, remove each mandazi and transfer to the paper towel–lined baking tray. Serve warm with a generous dusting of powdered sugar.

10

koko's pancakes

Thicker than a crepe yet thinner than American pancakes, Kenyan-style pancakes take after a European-style pancake that is tender and springy in texture. I could always convince my grandma (nicknamed Koko by her grandchildren) to whip up a batch if her chickens had laid eggs that morning. She likes to serve them with fruit jam for a touch of sweetness.

tip
Garnish with grilled pineapple to take your pancakes to the next level.

1⅔ cups (215 grams) all-purpose flour

⅔ cup water

⅔ cup whole milk

2 large eggs

2 tablespoons granulated sugar

2 tablespoons melted butter or neutral oil, such as avocado oil

1½ teaspoons baking powder

½ teaspoon fine sea salt

Neutral oil, such as avocado oil, or nonstick vegetable oil spray, for cooking

Honey or fruit jam, for serving

---

1   Place the flour, water, milk, eggs, sugar, melted butter, baking powder, and salt into a medium bowl and whisk together until there are no lumps.

2   Heat a wide nonstick skillet on medium heat and lightly coat the surface with oil. When the pan is hot, lower the heat to medium-low. Using a ¼ cup measure per pancake, pour the batter into the center of the skillet. Starting in the center, using the back of a metal spoon, spread the batter into a thin layer around 8 inches wide in diameter. Cook the pancake until tiny bubbles begin to appear and the edges look cooked, then flip and cook the other side until lightly golden, 1 to 2 minutes on each side. Transfer to a plate. Keep the cooked pancakes warm by covering them with a second inverted plate. Repeat with the remaining batter. Serve with honey or jam.

golden cinnamon rolls

There is no shortage of sweets in the American breakfast, but cinnamon rolls still feel special for some reason. My first departure from the American cinnamon roll was from a Swedish bakery where the dough was laced with coarsely crushed cardamom. Turmeric gives these rolls their bright yellow hue, signaling to the eater that these are no regular cinnamon rolls.

For the Dough

¾ cup warm whole milk

6 tablespoons unsalted butter, plus more for the pan

¼ cup (50 grams) granulated sugar

2½ teaspoons (1 envelope) active dry yeast

1 large egg, at room temperature

3 cups (390 grams) all-purpose flour, plus more for dusting

1 tablespoon coarsely ground cardamom

1 teaspoon turmeric powder

1 teaspoon fine sea salt

For the Cinnamon Filling

1 packed cup (200 grams) light brown sugar

8 tablespoons unsalted butter, at room temperature

1 tablespoon ground cinnamon

For the Cream Cheese Glaze

8 ounces cream cheese, at room temperature

1 cup (120 grams) powdered sugar

4 tablespoons unsalted butter, at room temperature

2 tablespoons milk

1 teaspoon vanilla extract or vanilla bean paste (optional)

1   **Make the dough:** Put the milk and butter into a small pot set over medium heat. Stir continuously and heat until the butter is completely melted, making sure it doesn't burn and the milk doesn't boil. Remove from the heat and leave to cool for 5 minutes or until it is safe to touch. If the liquid is too hot, it will kill in the yeast. Transfer to a liquid measuring cup and stir in the granulated sugar and yeast. Set aside until the mixture is bubbling, about 5 minutes.

2   Place the yeast mixture, egg, flour, cardamom, turmeric, and salt into the bowl of a stand mixer fitted with the hook attachment. Bring everything together while mixing on low speed. Once the dough begins to form, knead on medium speed until the dough is pulling cleanly from the sides of the bowl, 8 to 9 minutes. Remove the bowl from the stand

mixer, cover it with a clean kitchen towel or plastic wrap, and let it rise for 1 hour in a dark and warm place.

3   Grease a square pan or 9-inch baking dish with butter. Knock down the dough and place it on a clean, floured work surface. Pat the dough out into a rectangle. Using a rolling pin, roll it out into a ½-inch-thick rectangle.

4   **Make the cinnamon filling:** In a small bowl, mix the brown sugar, butter, and cinnamon. Spread the cinnamon mixture evenly across the dough and roll it up into a log. Cut into 9 pieces and arrange on the greased baking pan. Cover and let rise again, until they're almost touching, about 1 hour.

5   While the dough rises, preheat the oven to 350°F (180°C). Place the proofed rolls in

the middle of the oven and bake for 20 to 25 minutes, rotating once halfway through to ensure an even bake.

6   While the cinnamon rolls bake, prepare the cream cheese glaze.

7   **Make the cream cheese glaze:** Combine the cream cheese, powdered sugar, butter, milk, and vanilla extract in a medium bowl, and using a whisk or electric mixer, blend until smooth.

8   When the cinnamon rolls are golden brown on top, remove them from the oven and place on a cooling rack. Pour the glaze over the rolls while they're still warm and serve.

mango & ginger scones

Scones are one of those pastries that shouldn't need much planning. I learned how to make scones in my school's cookery club in London. A classic English scone is all about getting the texture right. The dough is a shaggy mess, but keeping the butter cold and dotted around the dough will yield a tender scone. Though scones can be made with fresh fruit, I prefer dried fruit as it won't mess around with the base recipe by adding extra moisture.

8 tablespoons cold unsalted butter

1 cup (150 grams) dried mango

⅓ cup (50 grams) candied ginger

2 large eggs

⅓ cup whole milk

1 teaspoon vanilla extract or vanilla bean paste

2 cups plus 2 tablespoons (280 grams total) all-purpose flour, plus more for dusting

⅓ cup (70 grams) granulated sugar

3½ teaspoons baking powder

1 tablespoon ground cardamom

½ teaspoon fine sea salt

Fruit jam, for serving (optional)

Clotted cream, for serving (optional)

1   Preheat the oven to 375°F (190°C) and place a rack in the center of the oven. Line a baking sheet with parchment paper. Place a medium mixing bowl, preferably metal, in the freezer.

2   Cut the butter into small ½-inch pieces using a knife or bench scraper. Place into a small bowl and freeze.

3   Chop the dried mango into small ¼-inch cubes. Finely chop the candied ginger smaller than the dried mango pieces, and set both aside.

4   In a small bowl, whisk together the eggs, milk, and vanilla extract. Remove 1 tablespoon of the mixture and set it aside in a small bowl for an egg wash later.

5   In the chilled medium mixing bowl, whisk together the flour, sugar, baking powder, cardamom, and salt. Add the chilled butter, and using your fingertips, break up the butter into the dry ingredients until it forms a crumbly

(recipe continues)

tips

Don't eat scones by themselves! This is a treat best enjoyed with a hot cup of chai, coffee, or tea. Or try it the British way, with clotted cream and fruit jam.

Bake them as you need them, as scones are best eaten the same day they are prepared.

Freeze a few, then bake a few! The scone dough will freeze raw for up to a month—just defrost thoroughly before baking.

STORAGE

Store scones in an airtight container at room temperature for up to 1 to 2 days, or in the refrigerator for up to a week.

mixture, similar to the texture of cornflakes. Stir in the egg mixture, dried mango, and candied ginger until a dough forms.

6   Lightly flour a clean work surface. Turn the dough out onto the surface and divide it in half. Pat each half into a 1-inch-thick circle.

7   Cut each circle into 6 pieces and place them on the prepared baking sheet. Make sure none of

the scones are touching each other or they will conjoin during baking. Using a pastry brush, brush the egg wash mixture on top of each scone. Bake for 15 to 20 minutes, or until they are lightly browned and no longer jiggly. Serve warm or room temperature with fruit jam and clotted cream, if using.

pumpkin bread with cream cheese glaze

Serves **9** to **12**

Pumpkin bread exists on that fine line between savory and sweet. It's something you can have in the morning with your coffee, or as an afternoon treat with a hot drink.

For the Pumpkin Bread

2½ cups (325 grams) all-purpose flour

1 tablespoon Baker's Masala (page 238)

2 teaspoons baking powder

½ teaspoon baking soda

½ teaspoon fine sea salt

1 (15-ounce) can pumpkin puree

2 large eggs, at room temperature

1 cup (200 grams) granulated sugar

¾ cup vegetable oil

For the Pecan & Pepitas Crumble

½ cup raw unsalted pecans

½ cup raw unsalted pumpkin seeds

¼ cup maple syrup

1 teaspoon sea salt flakes

For the Glaze

⅓ cup (70 grams) sugar

½ teaspoon Baker's Masala (page 238)

8 ounces cream cheese, at room temperature

⅓ cup heavy whipping cream

1 **Make the pumpkin bread:** Position a rack in the center of your oven, and preheat to 350°F (180°C). Grease a 9-inch baking pan with oil on all sides, and line the bottom with parchment paper.

2 Whisk together the flour, baker's masala, baking powder, baking soda, and fine sea salt in a medium mixing bowl. Set aside.

3 In a large mixing bowl, using a whisk, combine the pumpkin puree, eggs, and sugar until smooth. Slowly whisk in the oil. When

everything is fully incorporated, fold in the flour mixture until just combined.

4 Pour the mixture into the prepared baking pan and bake, 30 to 45 minutes, or until a fork inserted in the center of the bread comes out clean. Allow to cool on a rack to room temperature.

5 **Make the pecan and pepitas crumble:** Prepare a parchment-lined baking sheet and set

(recipe continues)

tip

Store extra slices in the refrigerator for up to a week.

aside. Roughly chop the pecans. In a nonstick saucepan over medium heat, combine the pecans, pumpkin seeds, and maple syrup. Bring to a simmer, tossing the pecans in the syrup to thoroughly coat them. Continue to cook, stirring occasionally, until there is no visible syrup pooling at the bottom, 3 to 5 minutes.

6 Pour the glazed nuts and seeds onto the prepared baking sheet, spreading them out so none overlap. Sprinkle with the sea salt flakes and allow to cool completely.

7 **Make the glaze:** In a large mixing bowl, whisk together the sugar and baker's masala. Add the cream cheese and beat with a hand mixer until smooth. Stir in the heavy cream and beat until combined and thickened, 2 to 3 minutes. Spread on top of the cooled loaf. Sprinkle the nut and seed mixture on top.

8 To serve, cut into 9 squares or 12 rectangles.

carrot sheet cake

Carrot cake, one of my most popular recipes, is what I call the "cake haters cake." It's moist, tender, packed with fruit, generously spiced, and nut-free. Baking it as a single layer sheet cake makes it easy to serve for a party, and also keeps a balanced cake to icing ratio.

For the Cake

1 cup (125 grams) raisins

2½ cups (325 grams) all-purpose flour, plus 1 tablespoon for the raisins

1 tablespoon Baker's Masala (page 238)

2 teaspoons baking powder

1 teaspoon baking soda

½ teaspoon fine sea salt

1 packed cup (200 grams) dark brown sugar

½ cup (100 grams) granulated sugar

3 large eggs, at room temperature

1 cup vegetable oil

3 packed cups (360 grams) grated carrots (using the small holes of a box grater)

1 cup canned crushed pineapple

For the Icing

8 tablespoons unsalted butter, at room temperature

6 ounces cream cheese, at room temperature

1 teaspoon vanilla extract or vanilla bean paste

1 cup (120 grams) powdered sugar

1   **Make the cake:** Position a rack in the center of your oven, and preheat to 350°F (180°C). Grease a 9 x 13 inch nonstick baking pan with vegetable oil on all sides and line the short side with parchment paper so it overhangs over the top edges; this will make removing the cake from the pan easier once it has cooled. Using 4 small metal binder clips, secure the parchment paper to the pan if needed.

2   In a small bowl, coat the raisins in the 1 tablespoon of flour.

3   In a medium bowl, whisk together the 2½ cups of flour, the baker's masala, baking powder, baking soda, and salt.

4   In a large mixing bowl, using an electric mixer on high speed, combine the dark brown sugar, granulated sugar, and eggs until the mixture is fully incorporated and light in color. With the mixer on medium speed, gradually pour in the oil and mix until thoroughly combined.

5   Turn the mixer down to medium-low speed and add half of the flour mixture to the wet ingredients. Mix until just incorporated, add the remaining flour mixture, and mix again. Be careful not to overmix or the cake will not rise properly. Stop mixing when it is nearly thoroughly combined and just a tiny amount of flour is visible. Add the raisins, carrots, and the pineapple with its liquid to the batter and fold in with a rubber spatula to incorporate.

(recipe continues)

tips

If you can't find canned crushed pineapple, blend fresh pineapple in a food processor and use with the liquid.

If you want to add festive decorations like sprinkles, add on immediately after frosting.

6   Pour the batter into the prepared pan and smooth the top with the spatula. Bake, 25 to 30 minutes, or until a fork inserted in the center of the cake comes out clean. Place the pan on a wire rack and completely cool the cake.

7   **Make the icing:** In a large bowl, using an electric hand mixer on medium-low speed, combine the butter, cream cheese, and vanilla extract. Once combined, mix on medium-high speed until the icing is light and fluffy, about 30 seconds.

8   Add the powdered sugar, ½ cup at a time, and beat on medium-low speed to incorporate each addition. It will be ready when all the ingredients are thoroughly combined and there are no lumps.

9   Use the overhanging parchment to lift the cooled cake out the pan and onto a serving platter. To decorate, using the back of a spoon, spread the icing over the top. For a neater presentation, transfer the icing to a zip-top plastic bag, cut off a bottom corner, and pipe it on top of the cake in any pattern you desire. Let the icing set before slicing.

chai cookies

A chewy cookie with a tingle of spice from the ginger. More often than not, I'm making a double batch and hoping it's enough.

16 tablespoons (2 sticks) unsalted butter

1 packed cup (200 grams) dark brown sugar

2 large eggs, room temperature

2 teaspoons vanilla extract or vanilla bean paste

1⅔ cups (215 grams) all-purpose flour

1½ tablespoons Chai Masala (see page 239)

¾ teaspoon baking soda

½ teaspoon fine sea salt

1 Preheat the oven to 375°F (190°C) and set the baking rack in the center of the oven. Line a shallow baking tray with parchment paper.

2 In a small saucepan, over medium heat, melt the butter, continuously stirring. Once melted, the butter will begin to foam and sizzle. Keep stirring, 5 to 8 minutes, until the butter has darkened and smells nutty. Remove from the heat and set aside to cool.

3 In a medium mixing bowl, whisk together the sugar, eggs, and vanilla extract until smooth. Stir in the browned butter. Add the flour, chai masala, baking soda, and salt and mix well with a soft spatula to combine.

4 Working in batches, using a cookie scoop (about 2½ tablespoons) or two spoons, portion out the cookies onto the prepared tray, leaving 3 inches of space between each.

5 Bake in the center of the oven until the edges of the cookies are set, 8 to 10 minutes. Remove from the oven and let cool. The centers will still be a bit gooey but will firm up more as they cool.

tips

Use a #24 cookie scoop to make nice big cookies!

For a bit of added crunch, sprinkle the tops with a generous pinch of raw sugar before baking.

chocolate birthday cake

It's highly likely that the chocolate sitting in your cupboard was grown in Africa. Brought to the continent by the New World colonists as a cash crop, West Africa is now the world's largest cocoa farming hub. Cocoa was grown to be exported and processed overseas—not for local consumption—but things are quickly changing as countries like Ghana are creating exciting culinary opportunities for the continent by producing their own chocolate products.

Dessert doesn't have as long of a history in many African countries as it does in Western nations, so it's not uncommon to find traditional European desserts, such as the British fondant-covered fruit cake, being served at weddings. Fortunately, the latest dessert trend has been a marriage of Western baking techniques that highlight ingredients grown on the continent's soil.

This celebratory chocolate cake takes the moist and airy texture of American-style cakes and pairs it with deeper flavors that highlight chocolate and coffee (one of Kenya's largest cash crops). Perhaps it's because sugary desserts are still relatively young in many African homes (my family included), but the biggest compliment for a dessert is "not too sweet!"

Trust me: it's the perfect treat for any celebration. This recipe is my ultimate dream birthday cake—festive, joyous, and not too sweet!

For the Chocolate Cake
2 cups (260 grams) all-purpose flour

1⅓ cups (270 grams) granulated white sugar

¾ cup (75 grams) sifted cocoa powder

⅔ packed cup (135 grams) dark brown sugar

1½ teaspoons baking soda

1 teaspoon baking powder

1 teaspoon fine sea salt

1 cup shaken buttermilk

¾ cup vegetable oil

3 large eggs, at room temperature

3½ ounces bittersweet chocolate (70% cacao)

1 tablespoon instant espresso powder

½ cup hot water

For the White Chocolate Frosting
12 tablespoons unsalted butter, at room temperature

4 ounces cream cheese, at room temperature

6 ounces white chocolate

1 teaspoon vanilla extract or vanilla bean paste

1 cup (120 grams) powdered sugar

Sprinkles of choice, for decorating

(recipe continues)

1. **Make the chocolate cake:** Position a rack in the center of your oven, and preheat to 350°F (180°C). Grease three 8-inch round cake pans using nonstick spray or oil and line the bottoms with parchment paper.

2. In a large bowl whisk together the flour, granulated white sugar, cocoa powder, brown sugar, baking soda, baking powder, and salt until well combined.

3. In a separate medium bowl, whisk together the buttermilk, oil, and eggs until combined. Make a well in the center of the dry ingredients and pour in the wet ingredients. Working from the center, whisk together, gradually incorporating the dry ingredients until there is very little flour visible.

4. Finely chop the chocolate and sprinkle on top in a single layer. In a small bowl, combine the espresso powder with the hot water and stir until fully dissolved.

5. Pour the hot espresso on top of the chocolate shards in the bowl. Allow to sit for 30 seconds, then, using an electric or handheld whisk, combine until smooth.

6. Divide the cake batter among the prepared cake pans. Tap the pans on the countertop a few times to make sure the batter is evenly spread and there are no large bubbles. Bake, 18 to 22 minutes, or until a fork inserted in the center of the cake comes out clean.

7. Allow the baking pans to rest on a wire rack until cool to the touch, then carefully remove the cake layers from the pans to finish cooling on the rack.

8. **Make the white chocolate Frosting:** In a mixing bowl, using an electric mixer on fast speed, cream the butter and cream cheese. Melt the white chocolate in either a small heatproof bowl over simmering water (double boiler) on the stovetop or the in the microwave in a heatproof dish. Add the melted white chocolate and vanilla to the butter mixture and, with the mixer running on medium speed, beat in the powdered sugar, a spoonful at a time, until the frosting is smooth. Transfer the frosting to a piping bag or, if using, a zip-top plastic bag and cut off the tip to make a ½-inch-wide opening.

9. **Assemble the cake:** Place a dollop of frosting on the base of a cake stand and use it to gently adhere the first cake layer to the stand. Pipe the icing along the top edge of the cake, then add more icing in the center and spread in an even layer. Add the second cake layer, flat side facing up, so the top is flat and repeat with the frosting, carefully spreading the rest of the frosting on top. Repeat with the third layer. Decorate with sprinkles.

Serves
8

green mango olive oil cake

When mangoes are unripe, they have a green skin and are quite firm. The tartness of the unripe mango works great in an olive oil cake, as it adds a bit of freshness without making the cake any sweeter. The taste of the oil comes through in this cake, so try to find an olive oil with a fruity flavor profile. This is where you should use the good stuff!

2 large unripe mangoes

1⅓ cups (175 grams) all-purpose flour

1½ teaspoons baking powder

½ teaspoon fine sea salt

2 large eggs, at room temperature

1 cup (200 grams) granulated sugar

1 teaspoon ground cardamom

1 cup (225 grams) extra-virgin olive oil

½ cup whole milk

2 tablespoons turbinado sugar or granulated sugar

Crème fraîche or vanilla bean ice cream, for serving (optional)

1. Preheat the oven to 350°F (180°C) with the rack in the middle of the oven. Grease and line a 9-inch springform pan with parchment paper.

2. Using a vegetable peeler, remove the skin of the mangoes. Save the flesh from half a mango for garnish. Grate or finely chop the rest of the flesh and put into a bowl until you get 600 grams of flesh plus juice. Set aside.

3. In a medium bowl, whisk together the flour, baking powder, and salt. Set aside.

4. Using an electric mixer on medium-low speed, combine the eggs, granulated sugar, and cardamom. It should start binding together but will still be a bit crumbly.

5. Slowly add in the oil and continue to mix on low speed.

6. Add in half the flour mixture and combine. Then add the milk, the remaining flour mixture, and the mango. Once fully combined, transfer into the prepared springform pan.

7. Sprinkle the turbinado sugar on top and transfer the cake to the oven, and bake, about 1 hour, or until a fork inserted in the center of the cake comes out clean and the top is golden brown.

8. Serve warm with crème fraîche or a scoop of vanilla bean ice cream, if using!

Serves
9

tip
Generously coat the tablespoon with nonstick spray before measuring the molasses.

sticky toffee pudding

Despite the name, this is indeed a cake that's served warm, and it arrives doused in a boozy toffee sauce. It's a cozy cake that is unabashedly indulgent. Typically served in the winter months, it's now a regular at all my holiday dinners. Borrowing flavors from South African malva pudding, half the dates are swapped out for apricots before being soaked in the nation's most popular tea. If you can get your hands on a bottle, try making the toffee sauce with Amarula, a fruity cream liquor.

For the Cake
2 bags rooibos or black tea

4 ounces pitted Medjool dates

4 ounces dried apricots

1 teaspoon baking soda

1½ cups (200 grams) all-purpose flour

1½ teaspoons baking powder

1 teaspoon Chai Masala (page 239) or ground ginger

½ teaspoon fine sea salt

4 tablespoons (½ stick) unsalted butter

2 tablespoons molasses (see Tip)

⅓ cup (65 grams) dark brown sugar

2 large eggs, at room temperature

For the Toffee Sauce
¾ cup heavy cream

8 tablespoons (1 stick) unsalted butter, at room temperature

½ packed cup (100 grams) dark brown sugar

½ teaspoon fine sea salt

2 tablespoons Amarula or spiced rum

1   **Make the sticky toffee cake:** Position a rack in the center of your oven, and preheat to 350°F (180°C). Spray a square 9-inch baking pan with nonstick spray.

2   Brew the tea bags in 1 cup hot water and allow to steep for 5 minutes, then discard the bags.

3   Place the dates, apricots, and baking soda in a blender or food processor. Add the hot tea, stir, and allow to sit for at least 10 minutes to soften the fruit, then puree until smooth.

4   In a medium bowl, whisk together the flour, baking powder, chai masala, and salt.

5   In a mixing bowl, using an electric mixer on medium speed, whip the butter and molasses until they are combined and slightly fluffy.

6   Once combined, add the sugar, mix to combine, then add the eggs one at a time, whipping the mixture between each egg until smooth. Mix in the blended date mixture until combined.

7   Add in the flour mixture all at once and mix on low speed until the flour is completely incorporated, being careful not to overmix.

8   Pour the batter into the prepared pan, spreading it into an even layer. Bake, 20 to 25 minutes, or until a fork inserted in the center of the cake comes out clean.

9   **Make the toffee sauce:** In a saucepan set over medium heat, combine the cream, butter, dark brown sugar, and salt, stirring until the butter and sugar have melted and the sauce reaches

STORAGE & REHEATING
Store any extra slices in the
refrigerator for up to a week.
Lightly warm in the microwave
before serving.

a boil. Once boiling, cook until thickened, 3 to 5 minutes. Remove from the heat and stir in the Amarula.

10 When the cake has finished baking, remove and place the pan on a wire rack. While it is still warm, use a skewer to poke 4 dozen or so holes all over the top. Pour over ½ cup of the toffee sauce and allow to sit for 20 minutes before serving. Serve with extra warm toffee sauce on the side. Enjoy!

apple & ginger hand pies

My mother always openly rejected fast food, but there were sometimes exceptions, and the McDonald's two for one dollar apple pies were one of them. When we'd be out late looking for a Kinko's to print off a school essay, she'd treat me to warm handheld pies filled with tiny cubes of apples. Store-bought puff pastry makes it feel like an any-time-of-day treat, resembling a morning Danish. I love to assemble a batch and freeze before baking. It's the best treat for yourself to always have a dessert on hand.

For the Apple Filling

4 crisp semi-tart apples, such as 2 Pink Lady plus 2 Honeycrisp

⅓ cup (60 grams) light brown sugar

¼ cup (50 grams) granulated sugar

½ teaspoon Baker's Masala (page 238) or ground cinnamon

½ teaspoon fine sea salt

⅓ cup (65 grams) candied ginger

Juice of 1 lemon

1 tablespoon cornstarch

For the Hand Pies

2 tablespoons raw sugar

1 teaspoon Baker's Masala (page 238) or ground cinnamon

¼ cup (30 grams) all-purpose flour, for rolling

2 sheets rolled puff pastry, thawed and refrigerated until ready to use

2 tablespoons whole milk or cream

1   **Make the apple filling:** Position a rack in the center of your oven, and preheat to 400°F (200°C). Line a baking tray with parchment paper.

2   Peel and cut the apples into ½-inch-dice cubes, discarding the core. Place the apples in a medium-size pot with the light brown sugar, granulated sugar, baker's masala, and the salt and mix to combine.

3   Set the pot on the stove over medium heat. Cook, stirring occasionally to prevent burning; the apples should release some juice as they simmer. The apples are ready once they have shrunk and softened, but still maintain their

shape, about 20 minutes depending on the variety.

4   While the apples are bubbling away, finely chop the candied ginger and stir it into the apples in the pot.

5   In a small bowl, mix the lemon juice and cornstarch until there are no lumps. Once the apples are at the correct doneness, add the cornstarch slurry to thicken up any residual liquid. Cook for another minute before removing from the heat. Set aside and allow to cool.

(recipe continues)

6   **Make the hand pies:** In a small bowl, mix the raw sugar and the baker's masala.

7   Lightly dust a clean work surface with flour. Working with 1 piece at a time, unfold the puff pastry. Using a rolling pin, roll it out a bit thinner, about ½-inch thick. Cut each pastry piece vertically into 6 even strips. Then cut across horizontally so you have 12 rectangles. Repeat with the other pastry piece.

8   Divide the filling among the 12 rectangles, leaving a ¼-inch border around the edges and being careful not to overfill. Using a pastry brush, brush the borders with the milk. Cover each apple mound with the remaining pastry rectangles, using a fork to press down and seal the edges of the hand pies.

9   Arrange the pies on the prepared baking tray, leaving an inch of space between each one. Carefully brush the tops and trim with the remaining milk, then sprinkle with the spiced sugar. Using a small knife, cut two slits for ventilation across the top of each hand pie. Bake, 20 to 25 minutes, or until they are a deep golden brown. Enjoy warm.

dirty chai tiramisu

Typically an "off the menu" item at coffee shops, a dirty chai is a hot spiced chai with a shot of espresso. The ladyfinger cookies absorb every drop of the dirty chai, so make sure it's a good pot of tea! Save the egg whites for another baking project like a Cali Mess (page 190), or whisk them with whole eggs for a breakfast scramble.

For the Cream

2 large egg yolks

2 tablespoons granulated sugar

1 (8-ounce) container mascarpone cheese

½ cup heavy cream

½ teaspoon Chai Masala (page 239)

½ teaspoon vanilla extract or vanilla bean paste

1 pinch fine sea salt

For the Dirty Chai

1 cup milk

4 black tea bags

2 teaspoons Chai Masala (page 239)

2 tablespoons Kahlúa coffee liqueur

1 teaspoon espresso powder

For the Tiramisu:

1 pack (24) ladyfingers

1 spoonful cocoa powder, for serving

1 **Make the cream:** Fill a saucepan with ¼ inch water and bring to a simmer over medium heat. In a medium-size heatproof bowl that is wider than the saucepan, whisk together the egg yolks and sugar. Once the water comes to a simmer, lower the heat to medium-low and place the bowl on top of the pot, making sure the water isn't touching the bottom of the bowl. Continue to whisk the eggs and sugar until the sugar has fully dissolved. Lower the heat as needed to ensure the eggs don't scramble. Using your fingers, test if the texture of the sauce is grainy or if the sugar has fully dissolved. The eggs will become a very pale yellow once they are ready. Remove from the heat, drain the water from the pot, and set aside to use again.

2 To the eggs, add the mascarpone, heavy cream, chai masala, vanilla extract, and salt, then using an electric mixer, beat the mixture on low speed. Slowly increase the speed until

(recipe continues)

the mixture is stiff, about 3 minutes. Cover with plastic wrap and chill in the fridge.

3 **Make the dirty chai:** In the reserved pot, combine the milk, tea bags, chai masala, Kahlúa, and espresso powder with 1 cup water. Set over medium heat and bring to a simmer, occasionally stirring to dissolve the sugar.

4 Remove from the heat, discard the tea bags, and chill to room temperature before using.

5 **Make the tiramisu:** Briefly dip the ladyfingers into the cooled dirty chai and arrange in a single layer on the bottom of an 8- or 9-inch serving dish. Carefully spread one-third of the cream mixture on top and repeat with two more layers of the dipped ladyfingers and cream.

6 For the top layer, use the back of a spoon to create a swirl pattern and then generously dust with the cocoa powder. Chill for at least 1 hour before slicing and serving.

cali mess

When you bake a lot, sometimes you end up with extra parts. If you make a custard for a pie that only calls for egg yolks, like the Passion Fruit & Lime Pie (page 198), you end up with extra egg whites. Egg whites can be stored in the fridge for longer than egg yolks, so whenever I have spare whites, it's time for a meringue! For whatever reason, I loved meringue cookies as a kid. I would always sneak a box of mint chocolate chip meringue cookies into the shopping cart until I eventually realized they were gross and tasted like toothpaste.

The Eton mess, an English dessert, is a trifle dish made of crumbled meringue, strawberries, and whipped cream. But more is more when it comes to dessert, and Californians can't shy away from an ice cream dessert! The best way to assemble is to make a little dessert bar so every guest can build their own mess.

4 large egg whites

¾ cup (150 grams) plus 2 tablespoons granulated sugar, divided

2 tablespoons lemon juice

¾ cup passion fruit pulp

2 cups strawberries

1 pint vanilla ice cream, for serving

Whipped cream, for serving

1   Position a rack in the center of your oven, and preheat to 250°F (120°C). Line a baking sheet with parchment paper.

2   Using an electric mixer with the whisk attachment, beat the egg whites on high speed until soft peaks form. Keep the mixer running and add the ¾ cup of sugar, a spoonful at a time. When the eggs look glossy, add the lemon juice, and mix to fully combine.

3   Spoon the meringue onto the prepared baking tray and spread out into a 1-inch-thick layer. Bake until firm, about 1 hour. Let cool to room temperature in the oven with the door open before removing it. Once cooled, break up the meringue into 1-inch pieces and transfer to a serving dish.

4   In a small pan, combine the passion fruit pulp and the 2 tablespoons of sugar and set over medium heat. Gently simmer until the syrup has thickened and the sugar has dissolved,

about 10 minutes. Transfer to a serving jug or bowl and allow to cool.

5   Chop the strawberries into ½-inch-thick pieces. Transfer to a serving bowl.

6   Set up your dessert bar with the meringue pieces, passion fruit syrup, strawberries, ice cream, and whipped cream. Set out small bowls or cocktail glasses to serve.

tips

Make the meringue up to 2 days in advance. Store the cooked meringue in an airtight bag or container at room temperature.

Make the passion fruit syrup up to 2 weeks in advance. Store the syrup in the refrigerator and enjoy any extra with your favorite desserts or ice cream.

You can find passion fruit pulp sold frozen in most Latin markets or large grocery stores. This recipe calls for half a 14-ounce bag. Fully defrost before use.

passion fruit & lime pie

Key lime pie is a classic American dessert, but sometimes the flavor can get a bit one-note. Passion fruit is tart, but once you add a bit of sugar, it makes for the most wonderful desserts. Gingersnaps instead of graham crackers make the base just as delicious as the pie filling, instead of it having a simply functional role.

For the Crust

200 grams gingersnap cookies

6 tablespoons unsalted butter

2 tablespoons granulated sugar

1 pinch fine sea salt

For the Filling

8 to 10 fresh passion fruit (¾ cup passion fruit pulp)

Juice (¼ cup) and zest of 3 limes

4 large egg yolks

1 (14-ounce) can sweetened condensed milk

For the Decoration

1 cup whipped cream

⅓ cup (35 grams) powdered sugar

Grated zest of 1 lime or seeds of 1 passion fruit, for garnish

1 **Make the crust:** Position a rack in the center of your oven, and preheat to 350°F (180°C).

2 In a food processor, pulse the cookies until all the pieces are smaller than a pebble and transfer to a medium-size bowl.

3 Melt the butter in either a small saucepan on the stove or in the microwave in a heatproof dish. Pour over the cookie crumbs and add the granulated sugar and salt. Mix well to combine.

4 Spray a pie dish with nonstick cooking spray, then spoon in the crust mixture. First, using your hands, distribute the crust mixture evenly, then using the flat bottom of a glass, gently press down along the bottom and sides of the dish until the crust is compact.

5 Bake for 8 to 10 minutes, or until the crust is firm and holds together. Set aside and leave to cool completely.

6 **Make the Filling:** Cut the passion fruit in half and scrape their pulp with a spoon into a food processor. Blend until the seeds have separated from the pulp, about 2 minutes. Strain through a fine mesh strainer into a bowl and use a spoon to push through the thicker pulp until only the seeds remain in the strainer. Stir in the lime juice and zest and set aside.

7 In a separate medium-size bowl, with an electric hand blender, beat the egg yolks until pale and fluffy. While whisking, slowly pour in the condensed milk until fully incorporated. With a spatula, slowly fold in the passion fruit and lime mixture until fully incorporated.

8 Pour the mixture into the cooled pie crust, and bake, 20 to 25 minutes, until it has mostly set; the pie should still wobble when you remove it.

9 Let the pie finish setting by chilling it in the fridge for 4 to 6 hours (or ideally overnight), until the pie is no longer wobbly.

10 **Make the decoration:** Before serving, spoon whipped cream onto the pie, dust with the powdered sugar, and garnish with freshly grated lime zest or passion fruit seeds.

tip

If you're in a pinch and don't have time to make your own passion fruit pulp, you can find it sold frozen in most Latin markets or large grocery stores. This recipe calls for half a 14-ounce bag. Fully defrost before use.

mango cheesecake

Serves **8** to **10**

Mango is the queen of tropical fruits. Yes, it's enjoyable on its own, but it surprisingly also pairs well with spice. This dessert is inspired by a drink from Dishoom, my favorite Indian restaurant in London, where they garnish their mango lassi with fennel seeds. In the US, we typically associate the taste of fennel with savory foods like Italian sausage, but that anise/licorice flavor works wonders to balance out sweetness. Keep in mind that cheesecake isn't a last-minute dessert, as it needs to be chilled overnight, so plan accordingly.

For the Crust

6 tablespoons unsalted butter

½ pound ginger cookies

2 tablespoons granulated sugar

1 pinch fine sea salt

For the Filling

32 ounces cream cheese, at room temperature

1⅓ cups (270 grams) granulated sugar

3 large eggs, at room temperature

2 egg yolks, at room temperature

2 teaspoons fennel seeds

2½ cups mango pulp (see Tip)

2 fresh mangoes, for garnish (optional)

1 **Make the crust:** Position a rack in the center of your oven, and preheat to 350°F (180°C). Coat a 9-inch springform pan with nonstick baking spray.

2 Melt the butter in a heatproof dish in the microwave.

3 Finely crush the ginger cookies in a zip-top plastic bag with a rolling pin, or in a food processor. In a medium bowl, mix together the cookies with the melted butter, sugar, and salt. Spoon into the prepared baking pan and using a measuring cup or glass, press it into an even layer. Bake for about 8 minutes, then remove and allow to cool.

4 **Make the Filling:** In a large bowl, using an electric mixer on medium-high speed, combine the cream cheese and sugar. Once smooth, add the eggs and egg yolks one at a time until combined. Finely grind the fennel seeds in a mortar and pestle or spice grinder. Add the fennel seeds and mango pulp to the bowl and whisk until combined.

5 Pour the cheesecake filling into the cooled crust and place in the center of the oven. Immediately lower the temperature to 325°F (160°C) and bake for 1 hour, until the top has set. The center may still be slightly wobbly. Turn the oven off and let the cheesecake cool inside the oven with the door cracked for 1 hour.

6 Cover the cheesecake with plastic wrap and chill overnight in the fridge before serving.

7 Dice the mango and garnish the top of the cake, if using, before serving.

tip

You can find mango pulp sold frozen or canned. If mangoes are out of season, these will be much sweeter than what's on the store shelves. If using fresh mangoes, peel, remove the flesh, and puree in a blender. Discard the seed.

chai

Maasai family members are notorious for asking, "Where's the tea?" before even saying good morning to one another. This milky-spiced black tea is arguably the essential drink in most Kenyan families. There is nowhere in Kenya you can't get a cup of chai. Well, maybe except in a bar, but I'm sure they'll fix you a cup if they have a kitchen.

The preparation of chai does take a bit of patience, as it's made on the stovetop. Chai can be consumed at any time of day. In the morning, it's incredibly delicious with something carb-loaded like fresh mandazi, warm pancakes, or even toast with butter and jam.

2 cups whole milk

3 tablespoons English breakfast black tea or 6 tea bags

3 tablespoons raw sugar

1½ teaspoons Chai Masala (page 239)

1   In a medium pot, combine the milk, tea, sugar, and chai masala with 2 cups water and set over medium heat. Bring to a boil, then cook at a boil until the tea has brewed and the chai begins to foam and slightly rise, 8 to 10 minutes. Do not walk away here! Just as a watched pot never boils, an unattended pot of chai is almost certain to boil over.

2   To serve, using a very fine-mesh strainer, strain out the tea leaves (or remove the tea bags, if using) into a teapot or individual glasses. Serve hot or cold over ice.

coastal mimosa

Maybe it's the orange juice, but mimosas always seem restricted to brunchtime. The tanginess of the passion fruit transitions this cocktail into an anytime bubbles cocktail, but I'm still serving this for brunch and through to the evening.

¾ cup passion fruit pulp (see Tip)

⅓ cup raw sugar

1 bottle (750 milliliters) chilled dry sparkling wine, such as prosecco, champagne, or cava

2 cups (16 ounces) chilled orange juice

Fresh passion fruit, for garnish (optional)

1   In a small saucepan, combine the passion fruit pulp and sugar and set over high heat. Bring to a boil, stirring occasionally, and simmer until the sugar fully dissolves, about 2 minutes. Transfer to a heatproof container. Once cooled, store in the fridge until ready to use.

2   Make sure the sparkling wine and orange juice are well chilled. When ready to serve, combine the wine, orange juice, and passion fruit juice in a large pitcher. Serve immediately, and garnish each glass with a halved passion fruit, if using.

tips

If you're in a pinch and don't have time to make your own passion fruit pulp, you can find it sold frozen in most Latin markets or large grocery stores. This recipe calls for half a 14-ounce bag. Fully defrost before use.

If you like your cocktails not too sweet, just halve the amount of sugar.

Serves

2

dawa

There are two types of dawa drinks: the boozy cocktail, and the cozy medicinal hot tea. The two drinks may have different ingredients, but they are both considered medicinal drinks, thus, the dawa *translates to "medicine" in Swahili. It's the kind of drink you'd crave when you're under the weather or want something warm without caffeine. Dawa doesn't always include spices, but they really give the drink that added warmth. My aunties are all believers in the medicine of dawa. If there is a cough or sniffle in the house, then there is a pot of dawa on the stove.*

½ lemon

3 green cardamom pods

1-inch piece fresh ginger
(see Tip)

½ garlic clove

1 small cinnamon stick

1 to 2 tablespoons honey

Candied ginger, for garnish
(optional)

1 Use a vegetable peeler to remove the zest of the lemon and then juice the lemon (roughly 2 tablespoons of juice). Using a mortar and pestle, crack open the cardamom pods. Slice the ginger into coinlike pieces. Using a mortar and pestle, crush the garlic and ginger.

2 To a pot with 2 cups water, add the lemon zest, cardamom, the ginger and garlic mixture, and the cinnamon stick. Bring to a boil, then lower the heat and simmer for 5 minutes. Turn off the heat and add the lemon juice and

the honey to taste. Stir until the honey has dissolved, then strain before serving. Garnish with a skewer of candied ginger, if using.

tips

There is no need to peel the ginger! Just make sure to wash it well before cutting.

Feeling good but caught yourself craving this? It can also be served over ice for a fun and refreshing summer drink!

DAIRY
FRESH MILK
FRESH MALA
CAKES
EGGS
UTENCILS
SWEETENED MALA

pili pili pineapple margarita

There isn't a bar in California where you can't order a spicy margarita. Pineapple juice rounds out the puckery cocktail adding a bit of sweetness while maintaining that element of tartness. Try to avoid the juices made from concentrate as they can be a bit too sweet and throw off the balance of the cocktail.

Scale the recipe up as you need and keep it in a pitcher next to a bucket of ice so your guests can serve themselves.

1 fresh medium hot chili pepper, such as serrano or Fresno

8 ounces tequila or mezcal

8 ounces pineapple juice

4 ounces fresh lime juice

2 ounces agave

Lime slices, for garnish

1   Cut the first third of the chili into thin slices and set aside for garnish. Cut the remaining chili in half and scrape out the seeds. Place into a pitcher and use a muddler to crush the chili. (If you don't have a muddler, use a large spoon.) Add the tequila and swirl for 30 seconds to infuse it with the chili. Stir in the pineapple juice, lime juice, and agave. Chill until ready to serve.

2   When ready to serve, use a slotted spoon to remove the crushed chili. Place the reserved chili and lime slices on a plate next to the pitcher for garnish and serve over ice.

watermelon juice

Watermelon juice is a refreshing stand-alone drink or an ideal base for a cocktail. I usually find it when traveling around Africa. Native to the continent, watermelon is a market staple on all corners.

Fresh watermelon

Fresh limes

1   Find the flat spot on the watermelon and rest it on a cutting board. Using a sharp knife, cut away the green rind and most of the pale-colored flesh, and don't worry if some of the white flesh is left behind. Cut into large chunks and add to a blender, working in batches so you don't overfill the blender. Puree the watermelon until smooth. Set a large sieve over a bowl. Pour the watermelon juice through the sieve to strain out the pulp and seeds, using a spoon to help keep things moving. Discard the seeds and pulp whenever the sieve gets clogged from the pulp.

2   Cut the limes in half. Squeeze in as much lime juice as desired to add a bit of tartness. Transfer to a pitcher and chill in the refrigerator until ready to serve.

tips

Use as much watermelon as your heart desires; a regular pitcher will take 4 to 5 pounds of watermelon flesh once it has been blended into a juice.

You can also use precut watermelon chunks, but the fresher the better!

For a supersmooth juice, strain using a fine cheesecloth to remove even more pulp.

my

jikoni

In Swahili, jikoni *means "kitchen," and these are the ingredients that I'm sure to always keep stocked in mine.*

oils/fats

Sure, you can steam and boil most foods, but fats are magical. They are an accomplice in changing the chemistry of your dishes to make them browned, velvety, and, most important, crispy! Not all fats are made the same; American butter will be less fatty than European butter, and a specific brand of olive oil may be more fragrant than another. So, as tempting as it is to grab the cheapest thing off your shelf, try to find something reasonably priced for you, but more significantly, that helps you create tastier food!

COCONUT OIL: Coconut oil comes raw or filtered. My preferred cooking oil is the raw form, which has a noticeable flavor from the coconut. It also has a high smoke point, which is great for pan-frying.

EXTRA-VIRGIN OLIVE OIL: In California, olive oil is found everywhere and is the primary oil I use in the kitchen. I always have a few bottles of California-grown extra-virgin olive oil in my pantry. Besides being perfect for salad dressing, I use it for low- to medium-heat cooking, baking, and oven-roasted dishes.

GHEE: Ghee is simply clarified butter, typically sold in jars. I infuse my ghee with spices (see page 235), making it an excellent cooking fat for simple pan-fried dishes such as steak, stir-fries, or seared salmon.

GRASS-FED BUTTER: Good butter can make a big difference in both flavor and texture. When shopping for butter, I prefer ones from grass-fed cows that are yellow in hue and higher in fat, like Irish or European-style butter.

NEUTRAL OILS: The neutral oil I keep on hand varies, depending on what I find (or what's on sale). The key thing to remember with neutral oil is to use ones with a high smoke point, so they can be used for medium-high to high-heat cooking, especially frying. Some of my favorites for general cooking are avocado and extra-light olive oil, and for deep-frying, peanut and sunflower oil are great.

NONSTICK BAKING SPRAY: A baker's worst nightmare is for the food to stick to the pan. Sure, you can butter and flour your baking dishes, but sometimes that can leave a residue on your baked goods. A nonstick baker's spray is no fuss and doesn't leave any weird gunk on your beautiful cakes.

RAW PALM OIL: A bright orange-red oil, raw palm oil is a staple in West African cooking. It is very sustainable in its production, and palm oil has a unique taste that is floral and earthy. It also gives any dish a distinct orange gloss that will surely stain your fingers and clothes, so maybe don't wear white when cooking with it.

spices

Dry seasoning is the secret weapon in any kitchen. However, quality isn't always the same, so here are a couple things you should keep in mind when purchasing spices.

Purchase in small quantities. Spices don't last forever and will lose flavor as they age.

Use single-origin whenever possible. Like your produce, spices taste different depending on where they are grown.

BLACK PEPPER: Despite being commonly paired with salt, black pepper is a powerhouse in the kitchen. I see black pepper as a star, so use it with intention.

CORIANDER SEEDS: Cilantro is a powerhouse plant, and its seeds may be the best part. When adding to savory dishes, I prefer these thin little spheres to be lightly crushed. They stand out in dishes where they first get to sizzle in a bit of oil.

CUMIN SEEDS: The whole seeds should always be bloomed in a dry frying pan before being ground up. If used whole, they love to be sizzled on their own in a bit of oil or ghee.

CURRY POWDER: Though curry leaves are a spice, curry powder is a blend of spices. Depending on the region of origin, the spices used will vary significantly. British curry powder, Jamaican curry powder, and Kenyan curry powder have their differences, so if a recipe calls for it, try to distinguish which style of cuisine you're preparing to decide which curry powder is best. I always keep Kenyan and Nigerian curry powder on hand. Kenyan curry powder can be purchased online. Nigerian and

Jamaican curry powder can be found in specialty West African and Caribbean grocery stores or online.

FINE SEA SALT: All my recipes call for this type of salt. If you cook with other salts such as kosher salt, you may need to add more, depending on the brand. Sea salt is excellent because it's relatively consistent in its saltiness, no matter where you're buying it from. In Kenya, it is the main cooking salt found in a grocery store of any size. Try to source salt that is very dry and fine in texture, as it's ideal for sprinkling evenly over food.

FLAKY SEA SALT: These thin salt pyramids are perfect for finishing dishes. Crush the flakes between your fingers as you sprinkle them onto steaks, roasts, and fried foods. My favorite brand is Maldon flaky sea salt from England.

GREEN CARDAMOM PODS: Inside these pods are lumpy dark brown seeds. Used in both savory and sweet dishes, cardamom has a distinct flavor. It's one of those spices you can use without going overboard. To remove the seeds, use a mortar and pestle to crack open the pods. The green pods are lovely to infuse into a liquid such as melted ghee for baking or milk for a hot drink. Crush the seeds into a coarse powder before use. There is rarely a need to crush them finely.

GROUND GINGER: I would never want to cook in a kitchen that didn't have ginger. Without ginger, there is no chai! I mostly use fresh ginger for savory cooking, but ground ginger can make any baked goods pop. Plus, the dried ginger adds a nice kick to spice blends without the heat of chilies.

KASHMIRI CHILI: This dried chili powder has a beautiful bright red color. The heat level is quite balanced and significantly less fiery than cayenne pepper. This can be found in any Indian grocery store.

PAPRIKA: Made from dried sweet red peppers, paprika is available in a few varieties. Good quality sweet paprika is a great way to add a mild flavor and some color to your dishes. Smoked paprika is my little cheat when preparing dishes indoors that would typically be cooked on an open fire. Hot paprika is commonly prepared as a blend of paprika and cayenne pepper.

flavor savers

I love going to specialty food stores to find new goodies to add to my pantry. Flavor-packed cooking bases and condiments can make any dish delicious with minimal effort. Chili sauces aren't just for the table but can also be used in all stages of cooking to layer in flavor.

CHICKEN/BEEF STOCK BASE: I prefer the Better Than Bouillon brand. Standard prepared containers of chicken stock are typically unimpressive, but I always keep on hand these stock bases, which are essentially concentrated stock. All you need to do is dissolve a spoonful into hot water and, voilà, instant stock!

ROSE HARISSA OR APRICOT HARISSA: I prefer the Belazu brand. Originating from North Africa, this chili paste is incredibly versatile. Use it as a stand-alone condiment or to add deep flavor and smoky spice to your cooking. Rose harissa has a mild floral note that isn't too perfumy, and apricot harissa has a sweetness on top of the smoky spice. Harissa is also a great way to spice up other condiments, such as ketchup and mayonnaise.

SHITO: An umami-rich chili paste from Ghana, shito traditionally pairs spicy chili with dried fermented shellfish. A jar of shito can save a bland takeout. Some newer brands offer both traditional and vegan versions.

baker's delight

Though home baking is frequently associated with special occasions, such as birthday treats and holiday cookies, my best baking is always done as an activity—same as any other hobby—and a well-stocked baker's pantry gives you the ability to whip up just about anything.

ALL-PURPOSE FLOUR: I use the King Arthur brand. Not all flours are the same. King Arthur produces a slightly higher protein all-purpose flour, resulting in a nicer structure to your

baked goods, especially the dough-based ones.

BAKING POWDER AND BAKING SODA: Both are leavening agents, giving lift and rise to your baked goods, making them light and fluffy. The rule to remember here is that freshness is key. Once aged, they lose their ability to make anything rise. I always try to buy small quantities of them (individual serving sachets), so I know they're always fresh. When in doubt, you can also test to see if they're still active—combine a ½ teaspoon baking soda in 1 tablespoon white vinegar or lemon juice, and ½ teaspoon baking powder in 1 tablespoon hot water. If there are no bubbles, its time is up.

DARK BROWN SUGAR: Molasses is what transforms plain white sugar into brown sugar. Many recipes call for light brown sugar, but I prefer to keep the dark variety on hand for a richer and deeper flavor. If you ever want to balance out the amount of molasses in a recipe, just swap out some dark brown sugar for white granulated sugar.

POWDERED SUGAR: Powdered sugar easily dissolves, making a smooth texture for glazes and icing. It can also be used for a beautiful presentation when dusted on top of finished baked goods.

RAW SUGAR: Also called turbinado sugar, this sugar's coarse and large crystals are not easily dissolved, making for a great finishing sugar. I add this to decorate unfrosted baked goods before baking, such as olive oil cakes (see page 184) and spiced cookies (see page 178), for a nice crunch.

grains and pasta

In many cases, grains are treated as if they're on the plate just to add bulk to a meal. However, in all African diaspora cuisines, you'll commonly find grains to be the star component of the meal. Grains don't have to be boring!

BASMATI RICE: This has always been the rice variety of choice in my household. Due to its thin grains, basmati rice cooks quickly and requires little liquid. I love using basmati rice in seasoned rice dishes because of this, whereas, with thicker rice grains, you may need to parboil the rice before using.

COUSCOUS: Couscous is made from wheat and dried for storage. There are two common kinds of couscous—the small granules (Moroccan style) and the pearls (Israeli style). Both are always in my pantry.

ORZO: Despite its ricelike appearance, orzo is indeed a pasta and needs to be prepared as such. Orzo is incredibly versatile due to its shape, and I frequently use it in dishes where I would typically eat rice. Orzo can be enjoyed at any temperature.

Meal prep has become all the rage, but I believe in the philosophy of element prep. Spending that bit of extra time creating homemade spice blends and condiments make flavorful meals a breeze. When making spice blends, use whole spices whenever possible for the best flavor. Toast the whole spices in a dry frying pan until fragrant, then grind into a fine powder using a spice grinder or mortar and pestle.

herby yogurt

Nearly any dish can be made better with a sauce. Herby yogurt pairs well with rice dishes or as a dip for fried bites. I prefer yogurt that is not too thick, and Indian or European-style yogurt rather than Greek.

Handful fresh mint

Handful fresh parsley

Handful fresh cilantro

1 fresh medium hot chili pepper, such as serrano or Fresno

3 garlic cloves

¼ cup lime juice

⅔ cup whole milk yogurt

Fine sea salt

1 Remove the mint leaves, discarding the stems. Roughly chop the parsley and cilantro (leaves and stems). Chop the chili pepper (remove the seeds for a milder flavor) into large chunks.

2 Combine the mint, parsley, cilantro, chili pepper, garlic, and lime juice in a food processor or blender. Pulse until it's coarse in texture. Add the yogurt and blend until it's bright green and smooth with no large chunks remaining.

3 Once finished, transfer to a serving bowl or storage container and season with salt to taste. Store in the fridge for up to 4 days.

mango sweet chili sauce

Like most fruit, when mangoes are overripe, they are both at their sweetest and their messiest. Besides making lovely smoothies, mushy mangoes can make a seasonally delightful condiment when simmered with sweet chili sauce.

1 medium very ripe mango

1 cup Thai sweet chili sauce

1 Peel the mango and cut into chunks, discarding the pit. In a blender, combine the mango chunks with ¼ cup water until smooth.

2 Transfer the mango pulp to a small sauté pan set over medium-low heat. Stir in the sweet chili sauce and simmer for about 15 minutes, occasionally stirring to keep the sauce from burning. The finished sauce should be shiny and thick enough to coat a spoon. Set aside to cool before storing. Store in the fridge in an airtight container for up to a week.

tip
If mangoes are out of season, you can find mango pulp sold frozen or canned, and these will be much sweeter than what's in the produce aisle.

pickled red onions

This is a quick pickle recipe that can be eaten immediately. It's great addition to heavier dishes such as braised meats that need something acidic to balance them out.

2 small red onions

1 cup apple cider vinegar

3 tablespoons granulated sugar

½ teaspoon fine sea salt

1 bay leaf

1 Slice the onions into ⅛-inch-thick rings.

2 In a medium saucepan, bring the vinegar, sugar, salt, bay leaf, and 1 cup water to a simmer over medium heat. Once it reaches a simmer, add the sliced onions and immediately turn off the heat. Allow the onions to sit in the liquid until cooled to room temperature.

3 Store in the refrigerator in a jam jar or airtight container for up to 2 weeks.

spicy tomato jam

I first made this a condiment for burgers to substitute for the "messy" ingredients: ketchup, onions, and tomatoes. Once this sweet and savory jam found its way into my fridge, it started finding its way onto all things between bread—breakfast wraps, burritos, and sandwiches—it brings life to them all!

2 pounds medium very ripe tomatoes

1 medium onion

1 packed cup brown sugar

¼ cup fresh lemon juice

2 teaspoons chili pepper flakes

1½ teaspoons ground coriander

1 teaspoon fine sea salt

1 Dice the tomatoes. Finely dice the onion.

2 Select a shallow, medium-size pot that will allow the jam to boil down properly and set it over medium-high heat. Put the tomatoes, onion, brown sugar, lemon juice, chili flakes, coriander, and salt into the pot and boil for 10 minutes.

3 Lower the heat to medium, stirring occasionally, and cook until the tomatoes have collapsed and the liquid has cooked off, 30 to 40 minutes. The jam is ready once it has darkened slightly and is glossy in finish—depending on how juicy the tomatoes are.

4 Decant into a clean jar and fully cool before closing. Store in the fridge for up to a week.

herby harissa

There are times when the best part of a meal is the sauce. Harissa is a North African chili paste that packs a ton of flavor and heat in each spoonful. It's worth finding your perfect harissa blend, then ensuring you are never left without it. Versatile and simple to whip up, this sauce can be used anywhere you want hot sauce or chimichurri; put this on meat, seafood, eggs, and vegetables to start you off.

2 handfuls fresh cilantro

2 garlic cloves

¼ cup rose harissa paste

1 lemon (unwaxed if possible)

Fine sea salt

½ cup extra-virgin olive oil

1   Finely chop the cilantro (leaves and stems) and place them in a small bowl. Mince the garlic and add to the bowl. Add the rose harissa paste, then the grated zest of the lemon plus 1 tablespoon of lemon juice. Season with salt to taste, mix well, then cover in with olive oil.

2   Store in an airtight container in the refrigerator for up to 5 days. Allow the oil to come to room temperature and mix well before use.

AfriCali

garlic ginger paste

Garlic is one of the best aromatics, but when combined with ginger, it becomes an even better base for nearly any savory dish. So much of Kenyan cooking is influenced by the nation's Indian population, and this combination is the starting point for most Kenyan-Indian dishes.

tip
To spare your fingers from smelling like garlic for the rest of the day, you can buy prepeeled garlic cloves in most supermarkets.

⅓ pound whole fresh ginger

⅓ pound (about 30) garlic cloves

½ teaspoon fine sea salt

1 Leaving the skin on, chop the ginger into ½-inch pieces.

2 Pulse the chopped ginger, garlic, and salt in a food processor until smooth. Store in an airtight container in the refrigerator for up to 1 week or in the freezer for up to 3 months.

peri-peri butter

Peri-Peri *is the word for spicy in Southern Africa—sometimes interchanged with* pili pili—*and you know it must be spicy because the name is said twice, so you don't forget. This compound butter packs some heat but is light enough for delicate seafood or grilled vegetables. It is best added toward the end of cooking, with a fresh squeeze of lemon juice to highlight that bright herby taste.*

Small handful fresh basil

Small handful fresh cilantro or parsley

4 garlic cloves

8 tablespoons (1 stick) unsalted butter, at room temperature

1½ teaspoons sweet paprika

1 teaspoon cayenne pepper

1 teaspoon fine sea salt

1 Discard the stems of the basil and cilantro, finely chop the leaves, and place in a small bowl. Mince the garlic and add to the bowl along with the butter, paprika, cayenne pepper, and salt. Mix well until combined.

2 Cut a 12-inch piece of plastic wrap or parchment paper and place it on the counter.

Spoon the butter mixture into the center. Wrap the paper or plastic wrap around it, and using the palms of your hands, shape it into a log, tucking in the ends when finished.

3 Refrigerate until ready to use. The butter is good for up to 1 week.

spiced ghee

Ghee, the Indian term for clarified butter, is a great kitchen staple due to its long shelf life and higher smoke point. However, this recipe is also inspired by some of the flavors in niter kibbeh, an Ethiopian spiced clarified butter. By clarifying the butter with spices, everything cooked with this ghee will also take on the taste of those spices. I love using this to make simple pan-fried dishes, especially with beef or lamb.

tip
If the ghee container is closer to 13 to 14 ounces, double the spices used.

1 container (6 to 8 ounces) ghee or clarified butter

10 green cardamom pods

1 teaspoon dried oregano

1 Scoop the ghee into a small heavy-bottom saucepan. Set aside the container to use later. Use a heavy object such as a mortar and pestle or a rolling pin to crack open the cardamom pods. Add the cracked pods and their seeds to the ghee. Set the pot over low heat, swirling to encourage the ghee to melt, and cook for 10 minutes.

2 Stir in the oregano and cook for another 5 minutes. Turn off the heat and allow the ghee to cool to warm or room temperature. Strain the ghee through a fine mesh sieve back into its original container. If the sieve has holes larger than the spices, line the inside of the sieve with cheesecloth. Store in a cool dry place.

baker's masala

butcher's masala

baker's masala

Spices aren't just for savory dishes; the right combination of spices can add warmth to your baked goods that sugar just can't do on its own. Add a scant spoonful of baker's masala to your cakes, pancakes, pies, and scones, or include it in any recipe that typically calls for cinnamon.

2 tablespoons ground cinnamon

1 tablespoon freshly ground cardamom

2 teaspoons ground ginger

½ teaspoon freshly ground black pepper

½ teaspoon ground turmeric

¼ teaspoon ground cloves

1 Combine the cinnamon, cardamom, ginger, black pepper, turmeric, and cloves in a small airtight container and mix well.

2 Cover and store in a cool, dry place.

butcher's masala

Butcher's masala is a versatile meat spice blend that works great as a seasoning for ground meat, stews, and slow-roasting meats.

1 tablespoon ground cumin

1 tablespoon ground coriander

1 teaspoon smoked paprika

1 teaspoon freshly ground black pepper

1 teaspoon ground turmeric

1 teaspoon ground cardamom

1 teaspoon fine sea salt

½ teaspoon ground cinnamon

1 Combine the cumin, coriander, paprika, black pepper, turmeric, cardamom, salt, and cinnamon in a small airtight container, making sure to mix well.

2 Cover and store in a cool, dry place.

chai masala

In Kenya, chai refers to all tea, whether it has spices or not. When spices are used, that blend is called chai masala. As a ginger-based spice blend, chai masala has multiple uses beyond preparing a pot of tea. Swap chai masala into any recipe that calls for a bit of ginger.

¼ cup ground ginger

1 tablespoon ground cardamom

1½ teaspoons ground cinnamon

½ teaspoon freshly ground black pepper

½ teaspoon ground cloves

¼ teaspoon ground nutmeg

1 Combine the ginger, cardamom, cinnamon, black pepper, cloves, and nutmeg in a small airtight container, making sure to mix well.

2 Cover and store in a cool, dry place.

curry powder

Curry powder is a spice blend found around the globe, with each nation having its combination of spices that can be used to make a curry. This version of curry powder combines East and West African curry powders, so it's versatile for various dishes.

2 tablespoons coriander seeds

1 tablespoon cumin seeds

1½ teaspoons fennel seeds

1 teaspoon chili flakes

1 bay leaf

1½ teaspoons ground ginger

1 teaspoon granulated garlic

½ teaspoon fine sea salt

1 Toast the coriander, cumin, fennel, chili flakes, and bay leaf in a small frying pan set over medium heat, stirring constantly so the spices do not burn. Once the seeds become fragrant and lightly toasted, 2 to 3 minutes, remove from the heat and transfer to a spice grinder or mortar and pestle. Pulse or grind until fine in texture.

2 Transfer the spices to a small airtight container, add the ginger, garlic, and salt and mix well.

3 Cover and store in a cool, dry place.

chai masala

curry powder

yaji (suya spice)

When you attend a Nigerian party, there are a few dishes you hope to find there. For me, that dish is suya. Typically arriving late with whoever was in charge of bringing them, these grilled meat skewers are generously coated with a peanut-peppery spice blend called yaji, aka suya spice. As a kid, the spice on the suya had too much (chili) pepper for my palate, so I would pass my suya over to my younger brother Timey who gobbled it up more aggressively than other foods.

Now one of my favorite pantry staples, yaji is not just restricted to grilled meat skewers but also a great pantry staple to wake up traditionally underwhelming dishes. This version is conservative on the heat, but if you love pepper, double up! When seasoning with yaji, pack it on. Generously coat your roast meats and prepare to see food fly off the bone! And always serve a little bit on the side.

½ cup raw shelled peanuts

2 tablespoons onion powder

1 tablespoon sweet paprika

1 tablespoon granulated garlic

2 teaspoons ground ginger

2 teaspoons freshly ground black pepper

2 teaspoons ground cardamom

2 teaspoons cayenne pepper

1 Using a powerful blender, carefully pulse the peanuts and grind them into a fine powder; overblending will result in peanut butter. Transfer the powder to a small airtight container and add the onion powder, paprika, garlic, ginger, black pepper, cardamom, and cayenne pepper and mix well.

2 Cover and store in a cool, dry place for up to 3 months.

acknowledgments

AfriCali is the cookbook I always dreamed of writing, and it's all thanks to my family, friends, classmates, and peers who have encouraged my cooking along the way. And to my bud, thank you for always making me feel like I can do anything and crush it!

Thank you, Mom, for taking me everywhere with you. By age ten, I was able to taste food from countries across the globe, from small mom-and-pop restaurants to extravagant seafood towers at your work dinners.

Thank you to my literary agent, Nicole Tourtelot. You came to me when I was ready put my on the dream of writing a cookbook on the shelf. Your persistence and dedication made this happen. Also a thank-you to Anna Worrall, who stepped in while Nicole was on leave and ensured that this book would be the best it could be.

Thanks to my editor, Justin Schwartz, and the publishing team at Simon Element. You allowed me to write the book of my dreams, instead of some other version that may have compromised my vision.

Thanks to my photographer, Kristin Teig, for being an incredible collaborator. Your talent and dedication helped bring my vision for the book to life, and working with you and David exceeded my expectations.

A special thanks to Tiana for being an amazing support. I couldn't have managed to create that many dishes in just eight days without you. Your culinary skills were invaluable, and your enthusiastic can-do attitude on set each day made each day of the book's photo shoot a damn good time!

A heartfelt thank you to Iszy. I am incredibly grateful that Akali introduced us. Despite the distance between us in London and South Africa, you went above and beyond to make this book the absolute best it could be. To-gether, we accomplished something truly re-markable. Thank you!

Thanks to my family, who always praised every dish I made since I was a small child. A big thank you to my Uncle Osborn, who called me the best chef even when I was barely tall enough to reach the counter. And thanks to my Aunt Tilly, with whom I have shared my passion for cooking and who has always made me feel confident in the kitchen. To my cousins Tei and Saruni, thank you for hyping up my desserts as the best on the planet.

Thanks to my siblings Alero, Timey, Orode, and Akali, who (almost) always had confidence in whatever I cooked for them. A special shout-out to my younger sister Alero for her eagerness to talk about food all the time, even down to agriculture. And to my baby brother, Akali, thank you for that cheerful grin every time I handed you a plate of food, even if it was just rice.

Thank you to my maternal grandmother, Anges Kiano Kasaine. Not only am I honored to share a name with you, but I also hope that one day I can make chapatis as soft and tender as yours. Your confidence in everything you do, from tending to your ranch to each meal you make, is truly inspiring. Your food will always be the best.

Thanks to my grandfather, who has always looked at me with joy and pride. And thank you for always asking to try whatever I cooked, despite the fact that you almost exclusively eat meals made by Grandma.

Thanks to my mom's siblings in Kenya, who have shown such enthusiasm for my cooking that they even stash away plates to keep for later.

Thanks to all my friends who have joined me at my dining table, and an even bigger shout-out to those who have hopped in the kitchen with me. Nikki, thank you for loudly enjoying whatever I cooked. Chlo, thank you for trusting me to feed you foods that you thought you hated. Emily, thank you for being my dinner party sous chef since our college Sunday dinners. Jasmine, thank you for being the hand model for my first self-published student cookbook when I was in London for grad school.

Thanks to my master's publishing classmates and London mates for your friendship during such an important two years that marked the beginning of my career in food media. Lizzie, thank you for coauthoring our Living for the Weekend cookbook, which went above and beyond our class assignment and will always hold a special place in my heart.

Thanks to Oscar for jumping in the kitchen with me for my London pop-up events, and for always being the most curious and adventurous dinner party guest. And Leo, thank you for introducing me to the marvelous culinary world of Ottolenghi.

Lastly, a big thank-you to all my friends, both old and new, who sat at my kitchen island while I recipe tested this cookbook. You were my invaluable test kitchen and made the process of writing this book feel like what cooking should truly be—a way to bring people together over a good meal.

I also want to take a moment to acknowledge Africa. For far too long, the world has turned away from what is on our tables. But now they are about to find out, and boy, are they in for a treat!

index

Vodka Chicken, Red Pepper, 112–13,
113